The Creoles of Louisiana

Jackson Square, New Orleans, formerly the Place d'Armes.

The Creoles of Louisiana

By
GEORGE W. CABLE

PELICAN PUBLISHING COMPANY
GRETNA 2005

Printed in Canada

Published by Pelican Publishing Company, Inc.
1000 Burmaster Street, Gretna, Louisiana 70053

CONTENTS.

LIST OF ILLUSTRATIONS.

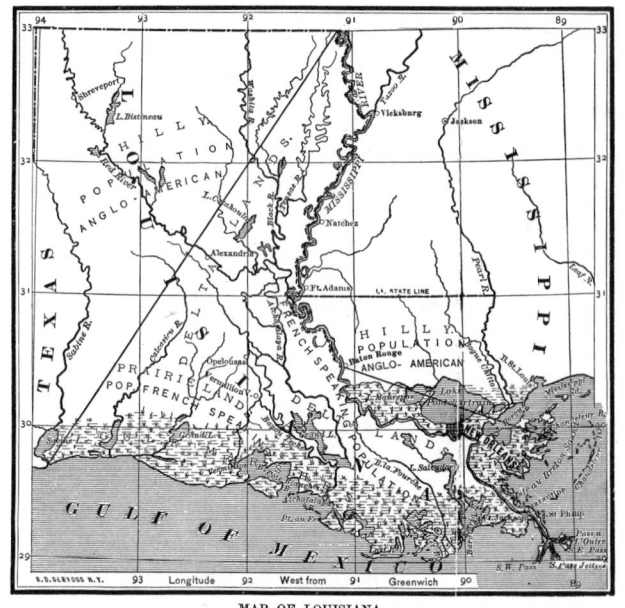

MAP OF LOUISIANA,

Showing, 1st, the country of the French-speaking populations, bounded on the east by the
Mississippi, on the south by the Gulf of Mexico, and on the west and northeast by arbitrary
right lines; and, 2d, the Bayou Têche running southeasterly through this region, and dividing roughly between the prairies, occupied mainly by the Acadians, and the Swamp country
adjacent to the Mississippi, the home of the Creoles.

THE CREOLES OF LOUISIANA.

I.

WHO ARE THE CREOLES?

ONE city in the United States is, without pretension or intention, picturesque and antique. A quaint Southern-European aspect is encountered in the narrow streets of its early boundaries, on its old Place d'Armes, along its balconied façades, and about its cool, flowery inner courts.

Among the great confederation of States whose Anglo-Saxon life and inspiration swallows up all alien immigrations, there is one in which a Latin civilization, sinewy, valiant, cultured, rich, and proud, holds out against extinction. There is a people in the midst of the population of Louisiana, who send representatives and senators to the Federal Congress, and who vote for the nation's rulers. They celebrate the Fourth of July; and ten days later, with far greater enthusiasm, they commemorate that great

Fourteenth that saw the fall of the Bastile. Other citizens of the United States, but not themselves, they call Americans.

Who are they?   Where do they live?

Take the map of Louisiana.   Draw a line from the southwestern to the northeastern corner of the State; let it turn thence down the Mississippi to the little river-side town of Baton Rouge, the State's seat of government; there draw it eastward through lakes Maurepas, Pontchartrain, and Borgne, to the Gulf of Mexico; thence pass along the Gulf coast back to the starting-point at the mouth of the Sabine, and you will have compassed rudely, but accurately enough, the State's eighteen thousand seven hundred and fifty square miles of delta lands.

About half the State lies outside these bounds and is more or less hilly.   Its population is mainly an Anglo-American moneyed and landed class, and the blacks and mulattoes who were once its slaves.   The same is true of the population in that part of the delta lands north of Red River.   The Creoles are not there.

Across the southern end of the State, from Sabine Lake to Chandeleur Bay, with a north-and-south width of from ten to thirty miles and an average of about fifteen, stretch the Gulf marshes, the wild haunt of myriads of birds and water-fowl, serpents and saurians, hares, raccoons, wild-cats, deep-bellowing frogs, and clouds of insects, and by a few hunters and oystermen, whose solitary and rarely frequented huts speck the wide, green horizon

at remote intervals.   Neither is the home of the Creoles
to be found here.

North of these marshes and within the bounds already
set lie still two other sorts of delta country. In these
dwell most of the French-speaking people of Louisiana,
both white and colored.   Here the names of bayous;
lakes, villages, and plantations are, for the most part,
French ; the parishes (counties) are named after saints and
church-feasts, and although for more than half a century
there has been a strong inflow of Anglo-Americans and
English-speaking blacks, the youth still receive their education principally from the priests and nuns of small
colleges and convents, and two languages are current : in
law and trade, English ; in the sanctuary and at home,
French.

These two sorts of delta country are divided by the
Bayou Têche. West of this stream lies a beautiful expanse of faintly undulating prairie, some thirty-nine hundred square miles in extent, dotted with artificial home-
stead groves, with fields of sugar-cane, cotton, and corn,
and with herds of ponies and keen-horned cattle feeding
on its short, nutritious turf.   Their herdsmen speak an
ancient French patois, and have the blue eyes and light
brown hair of Northern France.

But not yet have we found the Creoles. The Creoles
smile, and sometimes even frown at these ; these are the
children of those famed Nova Scotian exiles whose banishment from their homes by British arms in 1755 has so

often been celebrated in romance; they still bear the name of Acadians. They are found not only on this western side of the Têche, but in all this French-speaking region of Louisiana. But these vast prairies of Attakapas and Opelousas are peculiarly theirs, and here they largely out-number that haughtier Louisianian who endeavors to withhold as well from him as from the "American" the proud appellation of Creole.

Thus we have drawn in the lines upon a region lying between the mouth of Red River on the north and the Gulf marshes on the south, east of the Têche and south of Lakes Borgne, Pontchartrain, and Maurepas, and the Bayou Manchac. However he may be found elsewhere, this is the home, the realm, of the Louisiana Creole.

It is a region of incessant and curious paradoxes. The feature, elsewhere so nearly universal, of streams rising from elevated sources, growing by tributary inflow, and moving on to empty into larger water-courses, is entirely absent. The circuit of inland water supply, to which our observation is accustomed elsewhere—commencing with evaporation from remote watery expanses, and ending with the junction of streams and their down-flow to the sea— is here in great part reversed; it begins, instead, with the influx of streams into and over the land, and though it in-cludes the seaward movement in the channels of main streams, yet it yields up no small part of its volume by an enormous evaporation from millions of acres of overflowed swamp. It is not in the general rise of waters, but in

their subsidence, that the smaller streams deliver their
contents toward the sea. From Red River to the Gulf
the early explorers of Louisiana found the Mississippi,
on its western side, receiving no true tributary; but
instead, all streams, though tending toward the sea, yet
doing so by a course directed *away from* some larger
channel. Being the offspring of the larger streams, and
either still issuing from them or being cut off from them
only by the growth of sedimentary deposits, these smaller
bodies were seen taking their course obliquely away from
the greater, along the natural aqueducts raised slightly
above the general level by the deposit of their own allu-
vion. This deposit, therefore, formed the bed and banks
of each stream, and spread outward and gently downward
on each side of it, varying in width from a mile to a few
yards, in proportion to the size of the stream and the distance from its mouth.

Such streams called for a new generic term, and these
explorers, generally military engineers, named them bayous, or *boyaus:* in fortification, a branch trench. The
Lafourche ("the fork,") the Bœuf, and other bayous were
manifestly mouths of the Red and the Mississippi,
gradually grown longer and longer through thousands of
years. From these the lesser bayous branched off confusedly hither and thither on their reversed watersheds,
not tributaries, but, except in low water, tribute takers,
bearing off the sediment-laden back waters of the swollen
channels, broad-casting them in the intervening swamps,

and, as the time of subsidence came on, returning them, greatly diminished by evaporation, in dark, wood-stained, and sluggish, but clear streams. The whole system was one primarily of irrigation, and only secondarily of drainage.

On the banks of this immense fretwork of natural dykes and sluices, though navigation is still slow, circuitous, and impeded with risks, now lie hundreds of miles of the richest plantations in America; and here it was that the French colonists, first on the Mississippi and later on the great bayous, laid the foundations of the State's agricultural wealth.

The scenery of this land, where it is still in its wild state, is weird and funereal; but on the banks of the large bayous, broad fields of corn, of cotton, of cane, and of rice, open out at frequent intervals on either side of the bayou, pushing back the dark, pall-like curtain of moss-draped swamp, and presenting to the passing eye the neat and often imposing residence of the planter, the white double row of field-hands' cabins, the tall red chimney and broad gray roof of the sugar-house, and beside it the huge, square, red brick bagasse-burner, into which, during the grinding season, the residuum of crushed sugar-cane passes unceasingly day and night, and is consumed with the smoke and glare of a conflagration.

Even when the forests close in upon the banks of the stream there is a wild and solemn beauty in the shifting scene which appeals to the imagination with special

strength when the cool morning lights or the warmer
glows of evening impart the colors of the atmosphere to
the surrounding wilderness, and to the glassy waters of
the narrow and tortuous bayous that move among its
shadows. In the last hour of day, those scenes are often
illuminated with an extraordinary splendor. From the
boughs of the dark, broad-spreading live-oak, and the
phantom-like arms of lofty cypresses, the long, motionless
pendants of pale gray moss point down to their inverted
images in the unruffled waters beneath them. Nothing
breaks the wide-spread silence. The light of the declin-
ing sun at one moment brightens the tops of the cypresses, at another glows like a furnace behind their black
branches, or, as the voyager reaches a western turn of the
bayou, swings slowly round, and broadens down in dazzling crimsons and purples upon the mirror of the stream.
Now and then, from out some hazy shadow, a heron,
white or blue, takes silent flight, an alligator crossing the
stream sends out long, tinted bars of widening ripple, or
on some high, fire-blackened tree a flock of roosting vul-
tures, silhouetted on the sky, linger with half-opened,
unwilling wing, and flap away by ones and twos until the
tree is bare. Should the traveller descry, first as a
mote intensely black in the midst of the brilliancy that
overspreads the water, and by-and-by revealing itself
in true outline and proportion as a small canoe containing two men, whose weight seems about to engulf
it, and by whose paddle-strokes it is impelled with

such evenness and speed that a long, glassy wave gleams continually at either side a full inch higher than the edge of the boat, he will have before him a picture of nature and human life that might have been seen at any time since the French fathers of the Louisiana Creoles colonized the Delta.

Near the southeastern limit of this region is the spot where these ancestors first struck permanent root, and the growth of this peculiar and interesting civilization began.

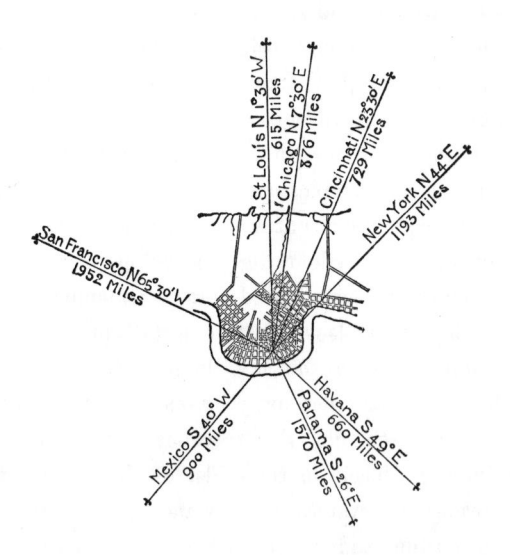

II.

L ET us give a final glance at the map. It is the general belief that a line of elevated land, now some eighty or ninety miles due north of the Louisiana coast, is the prehistoric shore of the Gulf. A range of high, abrupt hills or bluffs, which the Mississippi first encounters at the city of Vicksburg, and whose southwestward and then southward trend it follows thereafter to the town of Baton Rouge, swerves, just below this point, rapidly to a due east course, and declines gradually until, some thirty miles short of the eastern boundary of Louisiana, it sinks entirely down into a broad tract of green and flowery sea-marsh that skirts, for many leagues, the waters of Mississippi Sound.

Close along under these subsiding bluffs, where they stretch to the east, the Bayou Manchac, once Iberville River, and the lakes beyond it, before the bayou was artificially obstructed, united the waters of Mississippi River with those of Mississippi Sound. Apparently this line of water was once the river itself. Now, however, the great flood, turning less abruptly, takes a southeasterly course, and, gliding tortuously, wide, yellow, and sunny, between low sandy banks lined with endless brakes of cottonwood and willow, cuts off between itself and its ancient channel a portion of its own delta formation. This fragment of half-made country, comprising something over seventeen hundred square miles of river-shore, dark swamp-land, and bright marsh, was once widely known, both in commerce and in international politics, as Orleans Island.

Its outline is extremely irregular. At one place it is fifty-seven miles across from the river shore to the eastern edge of the marshes. Near the lower end there is scarcely the range of a " musket-shot " between river and sea. At a point almost midway of the island's length the river and Lake Pontchartrain approach to within six miles of each other, and it was here that, in February, 1718, was founded the city of New Orleans.

Strictly, the genesis of Louisiana dates nineteen years earlier. In 1699, while Spain and Great Britain, each for itself, were endeavoring to pre-empt the southern outlet of the Mississippi Valley, France had sent a small fleet from Brest for the same purpose, under command of the brave and adventurous Canadian, D'Iberville. This gallant sailor was the oldest living member in a remarkably brilliant group of brothers, the sons of M. Lemoyne de Bienville, a gentleman of Quebec, who had been able, as it appears, to add to the family name of Lemoyne the title of a distinct estate for six of his seven sons.

With D'Iberville came several remoter kinsmen and at

least two of his brothers, Sauvolle and Bienville. The eldest of the seven was dead, and the name of his estate, Bienville, had fallen to the youngest, Jean Baptiste by name, a midshipman of but twenty-two, but destined to

Bienville.

be the builder, as his older brother was the founder, of Louisiana, and to weave his name, a golden thread, into the history of the Creoles in the Mississippi delta.

D'Iberville's arrival in the northern waters of the Gulf was none too soon for his purpose. He found the Spaniards just establishing themselves at Pensacola with a fleet of too nearly his own's strength to be amiably crowded aside, and themselves too old in diplomacy to listen to his graceful dissimulations; wherefore he sailed farther west and planted his colony upon some low, infertile, red, sandy bluffs covered with live-oaks and the towering yellow-pine, on the eastern shore of a beautiful, sheltered water, naming the bay after the small tribe of Indians that he found there, Biloxi. The young Bienville, sent on to explore the water-ways of the country westward, met a British officer ascending the Mississippi with two vessels in search of a spot fit for colonization, and by assertions more ingenious than candid induced him to withdraw, where a long bend of the river, shining in the distant plain, is still pointed out from the towers and steeples of New Orleans as the English Turn.

The story of the nineteen years that followed may be told almost in a line. Sauvolle, left by D'Iberville in charge at Biloxi, died two years after and was succeeded by Bienville. The governorship of the province thus assumed by the young French Canadian sailor on the threshold of manhood he did not finally lay down until, an old Knight of St. Louis turning his sixty-fifth year, he had more than earned the title, fondly given him by the Creoles, of "the father of Louisiana." He was on one occasion still their advocate before the prime minister of France, when bowed by the weight of eighty-six winters, and still the object of a public affection that seems but his just due

when we contemplate in his portrait the broad, calm fore-
head, the studious eye, observant, even searching, and yet
quiet and pensive, the slender nostrils, the firm-set jaw,
the lines of self-discipline, the strong, wide, steel-clad
shoulders and the general air of kind sagacity and reserved
candor, which it is easy to believe, from his history, were
nature's, not the painter's, gifts.

It was he who projected and founded New Orleans.
The colony at Biloxi, and later at Mobile, was a feeble and
ravenous infant griped and racked by two internal factions.
One was bent on finding gold and silver, on pearl-fishing,
a fur trade, and a commerce with South America, and,
therefore, in favor of a sea-coast establishment ; the other
advocated the importation of French agriculturists, and
their settlement on the alluvial banks of the Mississippi.
Bienville, always the foremost explorer and the wisest
counsellor, from the beginning urged this wiser design.
For years he was overruled under the commercial policy
of the merchant monopolist, Anthony Crozat, to whom the
French king had farmed the province. But when Crozat's
large but unremunerative privileges fell into the hands of
John Law, director-general of the renowned Mississippi
Company, Bienville's counsel prevailed, and steps were
taken for removing to the banks of the Mississippi the
handful of French and Canadians who were struggling
against starvation, in their irrational search after sudden
wealth on the sterile beaches of Mississippi Sound and
Massacre Island.

The year before Bienville secured this long-sought authorization to found a new post on the Mississippi he had selected its site. It was immediately on the bank of the stream. No later sagacity has ever succeeded in pointing out a more favorable site on which to put up the gates of the great valley ; and here—though the land was only ten feet above sea-level at the water's edge, and sank quickly back to a minimum height of a few inches; though it was almost wholly covered with a cypress swamp and was visibly subject to frequent, if not annual overflow ; and though a hundred miles lay between it and the mouth of a river whose current, in times of flood, it was maintained, no vessel could overcome—here Bienville, in 1718, changed from the midshipman of twenty-two to the frontiersman, explorer, and commander of forty-one, placed a detachment of twenty-five convicts and as many carpenters, who, with some voyageurs from the Illinois River, made a clearing and erected a few scattered huts along the bank of the river, as the beginning of that which he was determined later to make the capital of the civilization to whose planting in this gloomy wilderness he had dedicated his life.

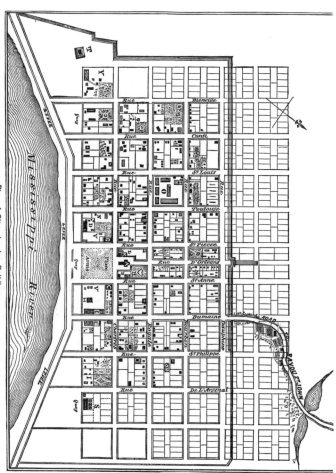

Plan of City, showing Buildings.

III.

THE CREOLES' CITY.

SCARCELY had the low, clay chimneys of a few woods-
men's cabins sent up, through a single change of
seasons, their lonely smoke-wreaths among the silent willow jungles of the Mississippi, when Bienville began boldly
to advocate the removal of the capital to this so-called
" New Orleans." But, even while he spoke, the place
suffered a total inundation. Yet he continued to hold it
as a trading post of the Mississippi Company, and, by the
close of 1720, began again, in colonial council, to urge it as
the proper place for the seat of government; and though
out-voted, he sent his chief of engineers to the settlement
" to choose a suitable site for a city worthy to become the
capital of Louisiana."

Thereupon might have been seen this engineer, the
Sieur Le Blond de la Tour, in the garb of a knight of St.
Louis, modified as might be by the exigencies of the frontier, in command of a force of galley-slaves and artisans,
driving stakes, drawing lines, marking off streets and lots,
a place for the church and a middle front square for a
place-d'armes; day by day ditching and palisading;

throwing up a rude levee along the river-front, and gradually gathering the scattered settlers of the neighborhood into the form of a town. But the location remained the same.

A hundred frail palisade huts, some rude shelters of larger size to serve as church, hospital, government house, and company's warehouses, a few vessels at anchor in the muddy river, a population of three hundred, mostly men —such was the dreary hunter's camp, hidden in the stifling undergrowth of the half-cleared, miry ground, where, in the naming of streets, the dukes of Orleans, Chartres, Maine, and Bourbon, the princes of Conti and Condé, and the Count of Toulouse, had been honored; where, finally, in June to August, 1722, the royal commissioners consenting, the company's effects and troops were gradually removed and Bienville set up his head-quarters; and where this was but just done when, in September, as an earnest of the land's fierce inhospitality, a tornado whisked away church, hospital, and thirty dwellings, prostrated the crops, and, in particular, destroyed the priceless rice.

The next year, 1723, brought no better fortune. At home, the distended Mississippi Bubble began to show its filminess, and the distress which it spread everywhere came across the Atlantic. As in France, the momentary stay-stomach was credit. On this basis the company's agent and the plantation grantees harmonized; new industries, notably indigo culture, were introduced; debts were paid with paper, and the embryo city reached the number of sixteen hundred inhabitants; an agricultural province, whose far-scattered plantations, missions, and military posts counted nearly five thousand souls, promised her its commercial tribute.

Then followed collapse, the scaling of debts by royal edict, four repetitions of this gross expedient, and, by 1726, a sounder, though a shorn, prosperity.

The year 1728 completed the first decade of the town's existence. Few who know its history will stand to-day in Jackson Square and glance from its quaint, old-fashioned gardening to the foreign and antique aspect of the surrounding architecture—its broad verandas, its deep arcades, the graceful patterns of its old wrought-iron balconies, its rich effects of color, of blinding sunlight, and of cool shadow—without finding the fancy presently stirred up to overleap the beginning of even these time-stained features, and recall the humbler town of Jean-Baptiste Lemoyne de Bienville, as it huddled about this classic spot when but ten years had passed since the first blow of the settler's axe had echoed across the waters of the Mississippi.

This, from the beginning, was the Place d'Armes. It was of the same rectangular figure it has to-day: larger only by the width of the present sidewalks, an open plat of coarse, native grass, crossed by two diagonal paths and occupying the exact middle of the town front. Behind it, in the mid-front of a like apportionment of ground reserved for ecclesiastical uses, where St. Louis Cathedral now overlooks the square, stood the church, built, like most of the public buildings, of brick. On the church's right were the small guard-house and prisons, and on the left the dwelling of some Capuchins. The spiritual care of all that portion of the province between the mouths of the Mississippi and the Illinois was theirs. On the front of the square that flanked the Place d'Armes above, the government-house looked out upon the river. In the corresponding square, on the lower side, but facing from the river and diagonally opposite the Capuchins, were the quarters of the government employés. The grounds that faced the upper and lower sides of the Place d'Armes were still unoccupied, except by cordwood, entrenching tools, and a few pieces of parked artillery, on the one side, and a small house for issuing rations on the other. Just off the river front, in Toulouse Street, were the smithies of the Marine; correspondingly placed in Du Maine Street were two long, narrow buildings, the king's warehouses.

Ursulines Street was then Arsenal Street. On its first upper corner was the hospital, with its grounds extending back to the street behind; while the empty square opposite, below, reserved for an arsenal, was just receiving, instead, the foundations of the convent-building that stands there to-day. A company of Ursuline nuns had come the year before from France to open a school for girls, and to attend the sick in hospital, and were quartered at the other end of the town awaiting the construction of their

Old Ursuline Convent.

nunnery. It was finished in 1730. They occupied it for ninety-four years, and vacated it only in 1824 to remove to the larger and more retired convent on the river shore, near the present lower limits of the city, where they remain at the present day. The older house—one of the oldest, if not the oldest building, standing in the Mississippi Valley—became, in 1831, the State House, and in 1834, as at present, the seat of the Archbishop of Louisiana.

For the rest, there was little but forlorn confusion. Though the plan of the town comprised a parallelogram of five thousand feet river front by a depth of eighteen hundred, and was divided into regular squares of three hundred feet front and breadth, yet the appearance of the place was disorderly and squalid. A few cabins of split boards, thatched with cypress bark, were scattered confusedly over the ground, surrounded and isolated from each other by willow-brakes and reedy ponds and sloughs bristling with dwarf palmetto and swarming with reptiles. No one had built beyond Dauphine Street, the fifth from the river, though twenty-two squares stood empty to choose among; nor below the hospital, nor above Bienville Street, except that the Governor himself dwelt at the extreme upper corner of the town, now the corner of Customhouse and Decatur Streets. Orleans Street, cutting the town transversely in half behind the church, was a quarter favored by the unimportant; while along the water-front, and also in Chartres and Royale Streets, just behind, rose

the homes of the colony's official and commercial poten-
tates: some small, low, and built of cypress, others of
brick, or brick and frame, broad, and two or two and a
half stories in height. But about and over all was the
rank growth of a wet semi-tropical land, especially the
water-willow, planted here and there in avenues, and elsewhere springing up at wild random amid occasional es-
says at gardening.

In the New Convent Garden.

Such was New Orleans in 1728. The restraints of social life had, until now, been few and weak. Some of the
higher officials had brought their wives from France, and
a few Canadians theirs from Canada; but they were a
small fraction of all. The mass of the men, principally
soldiers, trappers, redemptioners bound to three years'

service, miners, galley-slaves, knew little, and cared less, for citizenship or public order; while the women, still few, were, almost all, the unreformed and forcibly transported inmates of houses of correction, with a few Choctaw squaws and African slaves. They gambled, fought duels, lounged about, drank, wantoned, and caroused— " Sans religion, sans justice, sans discipline, sans ordre, et sans police."

Yet the company, as required by its charter, had begun to improve the social as well as the architectural features of its provincial capital. The importation of male vagabonds had ceased; stringent penalties had been laid upon gambling, and as already noted, steps had been taken to promote education and religion. The aid of the Jesuits had been enlisted for the training of the male youth and the advancement of agriculture.

In the winter of 1727–28 a crowning benefit had been reached. On the levee, just in front of the Place d'Armes the motley public of the wild town was gathered to see a goodly sight. A ship had come across the sea and up the river with the most precious of all possible earthly cargoes. She had tied up against the grassy, willow-planted bank, and there were coming ashore and grouping together in the Place d'Armes under escort of the Ursuline nuns, a good threescore, not of houseless girls from the streets of Paris, as heretofore, but of maidens from the hearthstones of France, to be disposed of under the discretion of the nuns, in marriage. And then there came ashore and were set down in the rank grass, many small, stout chests of clothing. There was a trunk for each maiden, a maiden for each trunk, and both maidens and trunks the gift of the king.

Vive le roi! it was a golden day. Better still, this was but the initial consignment. Similar companies came in subsequent years, and the girls with trunks were long known in the traditions of their colonial descendants by the honorable distinction of the "*filles à la cassette*"—the casket-girls. There cannot but linger a regret around this slender fact, so full of romance and the best poetry of real life, that it is so slender. But the Creoles have never been careful for the authentication of their traditions, and the only assurance left to us so late as this is, that the good blood of these modest girls of long-forgotten names, and of the brave soldiers to whom they gave their hands with the king's assent and dower, flows in the veins of the best Creole families of the present day.

Thus, at the end of the first ten years, the town summed up all the true, though roughly outlined, features of a civilized community: the church, the school, courts, hospital, council-hall, virtuous homes, a military arm and a commerce. This last was fettered by the monopoly rights of the company; but the thirst for gold, silver, and pearls had yielded to wiser thought, a fur trade had developed, and the scheme of an agricultural colony was rewarded with success.

But of this town and province, to whose development

their founder had dedicated all his energies and sagacity, Bienville was no longer governor. In October, 1726, the schemes of official rivals had procured not only his displacement, but that of his various kinsmen in the colony. It was under a new commandant-general, M. Périer, that protection from flood received noteworthy attention, and that, in 1726, the first levee worthy of the name was built on the bank of the Mississippi.

IV.

AFRICAN SLAVES AND INDIAN WARS.

THE problem of civilization in Louisiana was early complicated by the presence and mutual contact of three races of men. The Mississippi Company's agricultural colonial scheme was based on the West Indian idea of African slave labor. Already the total number of blacks had risen to equal that of the whites, and within the Delta, outside of New Orleans, they must have largely preponderated. In 1727 this idea began to be put into effect just without the town's upper boundary, where the Jesuit fathers accommodated themselves to it in model form, and between 1726 and 1745 gradually acquired and put under cultivation the whole tract of land now covered by the First District of New Orleans, the centre of the city's wealth and commerce. The slender, wedge-shaped space between Common and Canal Streets, and the subsequent accretions of soil on the river front, are the only parts of the First District not once comprised in the Jesuits' plantations. Education seems not to have had their immediate attention, but a myrtle orchard was planted on their river-front, and the orange, fig, and sugar-cane were introduced by them into the country at later intervals.

Other and older plantations were yearly sending in the products of the same unfortunate agricultural system. The wheat and the flour from the Illinois and the Wabash were the results of free farm and mill labor; but the tobacco, the timber, the indigo, and the rice came mainly from the slave-tilled fields of the company's grantees scattered at wide intervals in the more accessible regions of the great Delta. The only free labor of any note employed within that basin was a company of Alsatians, which had been originally settled on the Arkansas by John Law, but which had descended to within some thirty miles of New Orleans, had there become the market-gardeners of the growing town, in more than one adverse season had been its main stay, and had soon won and long enjoyed the happy distinction of hearing their region called in fond remembrance of the rich Burgundian hills of the same name far beyond the ocean—the *Côte d'Or*, the " Golden Coast."

The Indians had welcomed the settling of the French with feasting and dancing. The erection of forts among them at Biloxi, Mobile, the Natchez bluffs, and elsewhere, gave no confessed offence. Their game, the spoils of their traps, their lentils, their corn, and their woodcraft were always at the white man's service, and had, more than once, come between him and starvation. They were not the less acceptable because their donors counted on generous offsets in powder and ball, brandy, blankets, and gew-gaws.

In the Delta proper, the Indians were a weak and di-vided remnant of the Alibamon race, dwelling in scat-tered sub-tribal villages of a few scores or hundreds of warriors each. It was only beyond these limits that the powerful nations of the Choctaws, the Chickasaws, and the Natchez, offered any suggestions of possible war.

Bienville had, from his first contact with them, shown a thorough knowledge of the Indian character. By a pat-ronage supported on one side by inflexibility, and on the other by good faith, he inspired the respect and confi-dence of all alike; and, for thirty years, neither the sloth-ful and stupid Alibamons of the Delta nor the proud and fierce nations around his distant posts gave any serious cause to fear the disappearance of good-will.

But M. Périer, who had succeeded Bienville, though up-right in his relations with his ministerial superiors, was more harsh than wise, and one of his subordinates, hold-ing the command of Fort Rosalie, among the distant Natchez (a position requiring the greatest diplomacy), was arrogant, cruel, and unjust. Bienville had not long been displaced when it began to be likely that the Frenchmen who had come to plant a civilization in the swamps of Louisiana, under circumstances and surroundings so new and strange as those we have noticed, would have to take into their problem this additional factor, of a warfare with the savages of the country.

When the issue came, its bloody scenes were far removed from that region which has grown to be specially the land of the Creoles ; and, in that region, neither Frenchman nor Creole was ever forced to confront the necessity of defending his home from the torch, or his wife and children from the tomahawk.

The first symptom of danger was the visible discontent of the Chickasaws, with whom the English were in amity, and of the Choctaws. Périer, however, called a council of their chiefs in New Orleans, and these departed with protestations of friendship and loyalty that deceived him.

Suddenly, in the winter of 1729–30, a single soldier arrived in New Orleans from Fort Rosalie, with the word that the Natchez had surprised and destroyed the place, massacred over two hundred men, and taken captive ninety-two women and one hundred and fifty-five children. A few others, who, with their forerunner, were all who had escaped, appeared soon after and confirmed the news. Smaller settlements on the Yazoo River and on Sicily Island, on the Washita, had shared a like fate.

In New Orleans all was confusion and alarm, with preparations for war, offensive and defensive. Arms and ammunition were hurriedly furnished to every house in the town and on the neighboring plantations. Through the weedy streets and in from the adjacent country, along the levee top and by the plantation roads and causeways, the militia, and, from their wretched barracks in Royale Street, the dilapidated regulars, rallied to the Place

d'Armes. Thence the governor presently despatched
three hundred of each, under one of his captains, to the
seat of war. The entrenching tools and artillery were
brought out of the empty lot in St. Peter Street, and a
broad moat was begun, on which work was not abandoned
until at the end of a year the town was, for the first time,
surrounded with a line of rude fortifications.

Meanwhile, the burdens of war distributed themselves
upon the passive as well as upon the active; terror of attack, sudden alarms, false hopes, anxious suspense, further
militia levies, the issue of colonial paper, industrial stag-
nation, the care of homeless refugees, and, by no means
least, the restiveness of the negroes. The bad effects of
slave-holding began to show themselves. The nearness
of some small vagrant bands of friendly Indians, habitual
hangers-on of the settlement, became "a subject of terror," and, with a like fear of the blacks, fierce Africans
taken in war, led to an act of shocking cruelty. A band
of negroes, slaves of the company, armed and sent for the
purpose by Périer himself, fell upon a small party of
Chouachas Indians dwelling peaceably on the town's lower
border, and massacred the entire village. Emboldened
by this the negroes plotted a blow for their own freedom;
but their plans were discovered and the leaders were
executed. In the year after, the same blacks, incited by
fugitive slaves sent among them by the Chickasaws,
agreed upon a night for the massacre of the whites; but
a negress who had been struck by a soldier let slip the

secret in her threats, and the ringleaders, eight men and the woman, were put to death, she on the gallows and they on the wheel. The men's heads were stuck upon posts at the upper and lower ends of the town front, and at the Tchoupitoulas settlement and the king's plantation on the farther side of the Mississippi.

But turning a page of the record we see our common human nature in a kindlier aspect. Two hundred and fifty women and children taken by the Natchez had been retaken, and were brought to New Orleans and landed on the Place d'Armes. There they were received by the people with tears and laughter and open arms. At first, room was made for them in the public hospital; but the Ursulines, probably having just moved into their completed convent, adopted the orphan girls. The boys found foster-parents in well-to-do families, and the whole number of refugees was presently absorbed, many of the widows again becoming wives.

The Chickasaws and Yazoos became allies of the Natchez, and the Choctaws of the French. But space does not permit nor our object require us to follow the camp of the latter, to recount their somewhat dilatory successes on the Natchez hills, and in the swamps of the Washita, or on the distant banks of Red River under the intrepid St. Denis. The Natchez nation was completely dismembered. The prisoners of war were sent across the Gulf to die in the cruel slavery of the San Domingo sugar plantations. The few survivors who escaped captivity

3

were adopted into the Chickasaw nation; but even so, they qualified by repeated depredations the limited peace that followed.

In 1733, Bienville was restored to the governorship; but his power to command the confidence and good faith of the savages was lost. In 1735, aggressions still continuing, he demanded of the Chickasaws the surrender of their Natchez and Yazoo refugees, and was refused. Thereupon he was ordered to make war, and the early spring of 1736 saw New Orleans again in the stirring confusion of marshalling a small army. The scene of its embarkation was the little village of St. John, on the bayou of that name, where, in thirty barges and as many canoes, this motley gathering of uniformed regulars, leather-shirted militia, naked blacks, and feathered and painted Indians, set off through the tall bulrushes, and canebrakes, and moss-hung cypresses, and so on by way of the lakes, Mississippi Sound, and the Alabama River, to exterminate the Chickasaws. A few months passed, and the same spot witnessed another scene, when Bienville disembarked under its wide-spreading oaks and stately magnolias, the remnant of his forces, sick, wounded, and discouraged, after a short, inglorious, and disastrous campaign in what is now Northeastern Mississippi.

Bienville's years — he was still but fifty-six — will hardly account for the absence of that force and sagacity which had once made him so admirable and of such great value; but whatever may have been the cause, the colonists, in whose affections he still held the foremost place, found in him only a faltering and mismanaging leader into disasters, whose record continued from this time to be an unbroken series of pathetic failures.

The year 1739 saw the French authority still defied and the colony's frontier harassed. In September, Bienville mustered another force. The regulars, the militia, three companies of marines lately from France, and sixteen hundred Indians, filed out through Tchoupitoulas gate and started for the Chickasaw country, this time by way of the Mississippi. At the present site of Memphis, they were joined by levies from Canada and elsewhere, and Bienville counted a total force in hand of thirty-six hundred men, white, red, and black. No equal force had ever taken the field in Louisiana. But plans had miscarried, provisions were failing, ill-health was general, the wide country lying eastward and still to be crossed was full of swollen streams, and when the little army again took up the line of march, it actually found itself in full retreat without having reached the enemy's country. Only a detachment of some six or seven hundred Canadians, French, and Northern Indians, under a subordinate officer, moved upon the Chickasaws, and meeting them with sudden energy, before their own weakness could be discovered, extorted some feeble concessions in exchange for peace. In the spring of 1740 Bienville returned with a sick and starving remnant of his men, and with no better result than a discreditable compromise.

Ten years of unrest, of struggle against savage aggression, and for the mastery over two naked races, had now
passed.   Meantime, the commerce of the colony had
begun to have a history.   The Company of the Indies,
into which the Compagnie de l'Occident, or Mississippi
Company, had been absorbed, discouraged by the Natchez
war and better pleased with its privileges on the Guinea
coast, and in the East Indies, had, as early as June, 1731,
tendered, and in April had effected, the surrender of its
western charter.   The king had thereupon established between Louisiana and his subjects elsewhere a virtual free-
trade; a fresh intercourse had sprung up with France and
the West Indies; an immigration had set in from these
islands, and, despite the Chickasaw campaigns and paper
money, had increased from year to year.   At the close of
these campaigns, business further revived, and the town,
as it never had done before, began spontaneously to de-
velop from within outward by the enterprise of its own
inhabitants.

The colony's star was rising, but Bienville's was still
going down.   The new prosperity and growth was not
attributed, nor is it traceable, to his continued government.   As time passed on he was made easily to see that
he had lost the favor of the French minister.   He begged
to be recalled; and in May, 1743, on the arrival of the Marquis de Vaudreuil as his successor, he bade a last farewell
to the city he had founded and to that Louisiana of which
it was proper for the people still to call him " the father."

V.

THE NEW GENERATION.

WHEN, on the 10th of May, 1743, the Marquis de
Vaudreuil landed in New Orleans, private enterprise—the true foundation of material prosperity—was
firmly established. Indigo, rice, and tobacco were moving
in quantity to Europe, and lumber to the West Indies.
Ships that went out loaded came back loaded again, especially from St. Domingo; and traffic with the Indians,
and with the growing white population along the immense
length of the Mississippi and its tributaries, was bringing
money into the town and multiplying business year by
year.

Hope ran high when the Marquis was appointed. His
family had much influence at court, and anticipations were
bright of royal patronage and enterprise in the colony
and in its capital. But these expectations, particularly as
to New Orleans, were feebly met. There was an increase
in the number of the troops and a great enhancement of
superficial military splendor, with an unscrupulous getting
and reckless spending of Government goods and money,
and a large importation of pretentious frivolity from

the Bourbon camps and palaces. By 1751, every second
man in the streets of New Orleans was a soldier in dazzling uniform. They called the governor the "Grand
Marquis." He was graceful and comely, dignified in
bearing, fascinating in address, amiable, lavish, fond of
pleasure, and, with his marchioness, during the twelve
years of his sojourn in Louisiana, maintained the little
colonial court with great pomp and dissipation.

Otherwise the period was of a quiet, formative sort,
and the few stimulants to growth offered by Government
overshot the town and fell to the agricultural grantees.
The production of tobacco and myrtle-wax was encouraged, but it was also taxed. Through the Jesuit fathers,
sugar-cane was introduced. But one boon continued to
eclipse all the rest: year by year came the casket-girls,
and were given in marriage to the soldiers chosen for
good conduct, with a tract of land to begin life on. The
last ship-load came ashore in 1751.

The most conspicuous attentions offered New Orleans
were a prohibition against trading with the English and
Dutch, and further inundations of paper money. The
little port continued to grow, though pirates infested the
Gulf, British privateers were sometimes at the very
mouth of the river, seasons were adverse, and Indian allies
insolent. It was reported with pride, that forty-five
brick houses were erected between the autumns of 1749
and 1752.

Among the people a transmutation was going on.

French fathers were moving aside to make room for
Creole sons. The life of the seniors had been what the
life of redemptioners and liberated convicts, combining
with that of a French and Swiss line and staff in and
about the outposts of such a frontier, might be : idle,
thriftless, gallant, bold, rude, free, and scornful of labor,
which the company had brought into permanent contempt
by the introduction of African slaves. In this atmosphere they had brought up their children. Now these
children were taking their parents' places, and with Latin
ductility were conforming to the mold of their nearest
surroundings. They differed from their transatlantic stock
much as the face of nature in Louisiana differed from that
in France. A soil of unlimited fertility became, through
slavery, not an incentive to industry, but a promise of un-
earned plenty. A luxurious and enervating climate joined
its influence with this condition to debase even the Gallic
love of pleasure to an unambitious apathy and an untrained
sensuality. The courteous manners of France were
largely retained ; but the habit of commanding a dull and
abject slave class, over which a " black code " gave every
white man full powers of police, induced a certain fierce
imperiousness of will and temper ; while that proud love
of freedom, so pervasive throughout the American wilderness, rose at times to an attitude of arrogant superiority
over all constraint, and became the occasion of harsh comment in the reports sent to France by the officers of their
king. In the lakes, canebrakes, and swamps, and on the

bayou ridges, of their dark, wet forests, and on the sunny
expanses of their marshes, a great abundance of bears,
panthers, deer, swan, geese, and lesser game gave a bold
zest to arduous sport. The chase became almost the only.
form of exertion, and woodcraft often the only education.

As for the gentler sex, catching less grossness from
negro slavery and less rudeness from the wilderness, they
were, in mind as well as morals, superior to the men.
They could read and write and make a little music. Such
French vivacity as still remained chose the ball-room as
their chief delight, while the gaming-table was the indoor
passion of the men. Unrestrained, proud, intrepid, self-
reliant, rudely voluptuous, of a high intellectual order,
yet uneducated, unreasoning, impulsive, and inflammable
—such was the first native-born generation of Franco-
Louisianians.

VI.

THE FIRST CREOLES.

WHAT is a Creole? Even in Louisiana the question would be variously answered.[1] The title did not here first belong to the descendants of Spanish, but of French settlers. But such a meaning implied a certain excellence of origin, and so came early to include any native, of French or Spanish descent by either parent, whose non-alliance with the slave race entitled him to social rank. Later, the term was adopted by—not conceded to—the natives of mixed blood, and is still so used among themselves. At length the spirit of commerce

---

[1] As to the etymology of the word there are many conjectures, but few bold assertions. Is it Spanish?—Italian?—Carib?—an invention of West Indian Spanish conquerors? None of these questions meet an answer in the form of hearty assertion. In the American Journal of Philology (October, 1882), Professor Harrison, of Washington and Lee University, Virginia, after exhausting Littré on the subject, says of Skeat, that "He proceeds with agile pen—dashes, abbreviations, equation lines—to deduce the word, though with many misgivings, from the Spanish *criollo*, a native of America or the West Indies; a corrupt word made by the negroes, said to be a contraction of *criadillo*, diminutive of *criado*—one educated, instructed or bred up, pp. of *criar*, lit. to create, also to nurse, instruct."

saw the money value of so honored a title, and broadened
its meaning to take in any creature or thing of variety or
manufacture peculiar to Louisiana that might become an
object of sale : as Creole ponies, chickens, cows, shoes,
eggs, wagons, baskets, cabbages, negroes, etc.   Yet the
Creoles proper will not share their distinction with the
worthy "Acadian." He is a Creole only by courtesy,
and in the second person singular. Besides French and
Spanish, there are even, for convenience of speech, "colored" Creoles; but there are no Italian, or Sicilian, nor
any English, Scotch, Irish, or "Yankee" Creoles, unless
of parentage married into, and themselves thoroughly
proselyted in, Creole society. Neither Spanish nor American domination has taken from the Creoles their French
vernacular. This, also, is part of their title ; and, in fine,
there seems to be no more serviceable definition of the
Creoles of Louisiana than this: that they are the French-
speaking, native portion of the ruling class.

There is no need to distinguish between the higher and
humbler grades of those from whom they sprang. A few
settlers only were persons of rank and station. Many
were the children of the casket-girls, and many were of
such stock as society pronounces less than nothing ; yet,
in view of that state of society which the French revolution later overturned, any present overplus of honor may
as well fall to the children of those who filled the prisons
before, as of those who filled them during that bloody
convulsion.

Old Villa on Bayou St. John.

In the days of De Vaudreuil, the dwellings of the better class that had stood at first on the immediate front
of the town, or on the first street behind, seem to have
drawn back a square or two. They were also spreading
toward and out through a gate in the palisade wall near
its north corner. Bayou Road, now a street of the city,
issued from this gate northward to the village and bayou
of St. John. Along this suburban way, surrounded by
broad grounds, deeply shaded with live-oaks, magnolias,
and other evergreen forest trees, and often having behind
them plantations of indigo or myrtle, rose the wide, red-
roofed, but severely plain dwellings of the rich, generally
of one or one and a half stories, but raised on pillars
often fifteen feet from the ground, and surrounded by
wide verandas.

In the lofty halls and spacious drawing-rooms of these
homes—frequently, too, in the heart of the town, in the
houses of the humblest exterior, their low, single-story
wooden or brick walls rising from a ground but partly
drained even of its storm water, infested with reptile life
and frequently overflowed—was beginning to be shown a
splendor of dress and personal adornment hardly in harmony with the rude simplicity of apartments and furniture, and scarcely to be expected in a town of unpaved,
unlighted, and often impassable streets, surrounded by
swamps and morasses on one of the wildest of American
frontiers.

Slaves—not always or generally the dull, ill-featured

Congo or fierce Banbara, imported for the plantations, but comely Yaloff and Mandingo boys and girls, the shapelier for their scanty dress—waited on every caprice, whether good or ill, and dropped themselves down in the corridors and on the verandas for stolen naps among the dogs, and whips and saddles, in such odd moments of day or night as found their masters and mistresses tired of being served. New Orleans had been the one colonized spot in the Delta where slaves were few, but now they rapidly became numerous, and black domestic service made it easy for the Creoles to emulate the ostentatious living of the colonial officials.

To their bad example in living, these dignitaries, almost without exception, added that of corruption in office. Governors, royal commissaries, post-commandants,—the Marchioness de Vaudreuil conspicuously,—and many lesser ones, stood boldly accusing and accused of the grossest and the pettiest misdemeanors. Doubtless the corruption was exaggerated ; yet the testimony is official, abundant, and corroborative, and is verified in the ruinous expenses which at length drove France to abandon the maintenance and sovereignty of the colony she had mis-governed for sixty-three years.

Meanwhile, public morals were debased ; idleness and intemperance were general ; speculation in the depreciated paper money which flooded the colony became the principal business, and insolvency the common condition.

Religion and education made poor headway. Almost

Old Canal in Dauphine Street.

the only item in their history is a "war of the Jesuits and
Capuchins." Its "acrimonious writings, squibs, and pas-
quinades" made much heat for years. Its satirical songs
were heard, it appears, in the drawing-rooms as well as in
the street; for the fair sex took sides in it with lively
zeal. In July, 1763, the Capuchins were left masters of
the field. The decree of the French parliament had the
year before ordered the Jesuits' expulsion from the
realm; their wide plantations just beyond the town wall
being desirable, the Creole "Superior Council" became
bold, and the lands already described as the site of the
richest district in the present New Orleans were confiscated and sold for $180,000.

In this same year, a flag, not seen there before, began
to appear in the yellow harbor of New Orleans. In February, a treaty between England, France, and Spain, gave
Great Britain all that immense part of the Mississippi
Valley east of the river and north of Orleans Island. The
Delta remained to France and to her still vast province of
Louisiana. The navigation of the Mississippi was made
free to the subjects of both empires alike. Trade with
British vessels was forbidden the French colonies; yet a
lively commerce soon sprang up with them at a point just
above the plantations of the dispossessed Jesuits, afterward the river front of the city of Lafayette, and now of
the Fourth District of New Orleans. Here numerous
trading vessels, sailing under the British flag, ascending
the river and passing the town on the pretext of visiting

4

the new British posts of Manchac and Baton Rouge,
tied to the waterside willows and carried on a commerce
with the merchants of the post they had just passed by.

The corrupt authorities winked at a practice that
brought wealth to all, and the getting of honest rights by
disingenuous and dishonest courses became the justified
habit of the highest classes and the leading minds. The
slave trade, too, received an unfortunate stimulus: a large
business was done at this so-called "Little Manchac," in
Guinea negroes, whom the colonists bought of the English.

The governor of Louisiana at this time was Kerlerec, a
distinguished captain in the French navy. He had succeeded the Marquis in 1753, and had now governed the
province for ten years. But he had lately received orders
to return to France and render account of his conduct in
office. A work of retrenchment was begun. The troops
were reduced to three hundred. In June, a M. d'Abbadie landed in New Orleans, commissioned to succeed the
governor under the shorn honors and semi-commercial
title of director-general. Kerlerec, sailing to France, was
cast into the Bastile and " died of grief shortly after his
release."

The Creoles noted, with much agitation, these and
other symptoms of some unrevealed design to alter their
political condition. By and by, rumor of what had secretly been transacted began to reach their ears in the
most offensive shape. Yet, for a time, M. d'Abbadie

himself remained officially as uninformed as they; and it was only in October, 1754, twenty-three months after the signing of a secret act at Fontainebleau, that the authoritative announcement reached New Orleans of her cession, with all of French Louisiana, to the King of Spain.

Such is the origin, surrounding influences, and resulting character and life of the earliest Creoles of Louisiana. With many influences against them, they rose from a chaotic condition below the plane of social order to the station of a proud, freedom-loving, agricultural, and commercial people, who were now about to strike the first armed blow ever aimed by Americans against a royal decree.

Their descendants would be a community still more unique than they are, had they not the world-wide trait of a pride of ancestry. But they might as easily be excused for boasting of other things which they have overlooked. A pride of ascent would be as well grounded; and it will be pleasant to show in later chapters that the decadence imputed to them, sometimes even by themselves, has no foundation in fact, but that their course, instead, has been, in the main, upward from first to last, and so continues to-day.

VII.

PRAYING TO THE KING.

A SINGLE paragraph in recapitulation.

In 1699, France, by the hand of her gallant sailor, D'Iberville, founded the province of Louisiana. In 1718, his brother, Bienville, laid out the little parallelogram of streets and ditches, and palisaded lots which formed New Orleans. Here, amid the willow-jungles of the Mississippi's low banks, under the glaring sunshine of bayou clearings, in the dark shadows of the Delta's wet forests, the Louisiana Creoles came into existence—valorous, unlettered, and unrestrained, as military outpost life in such a land might make them. In sentiment they were loyal to their king; in principle, to themselves and their soil. Sixty-three years had passed, with floods and famines and Indian wars, corrupt misgovernment and its resultant distresses, when in 1762 it suited the schemes of an unprincipled court secretly to convey the unprofitable colony —land and people, all and singular—to the King of Spain.

In the early summer of 1764, before the news of this unfeeling barter had startled the ears of the colonists, a certain class in New Orleans had begun to make formal complaint of a condition of affairs in their sorry little town (commercial and financial rather than political) that seemed to them no longer bearable. There had been commercial development; but, in the light of their grievances, this only showed through what a débris of public disorder the commerce of a country or town may make a certain progress.

These petitioners were the merchants of New Orleans. Their voice was now heard for the first time. The private material interests of the town and the oppressions of two corrupt governments were soon to come to an open struggle. It was to end, for the Creoles, in ignominy and disaster. But in better years further on there was a time in store when arms should no longer overawe; but when commerce, instead, was to rule the destinies, not of a French or Spanish military post, but of the great southern sea-port of a nation yet to be. Meanwhile the spirit of independence was stirring within the inhabitants. They scarcely half recognized it themselves (there is a certain unconsciousness in truth and right); but their director-general's zeal for royalty was chafed.

" As I was finishing this letter," wrote M. d'Abbadie, " the merchants of New Orleans presented me with a petition, a copy of which I have the honor to forward. You will find in it those characteristic features of sedition and insubordination of which I complain."

A few months later came word of the cession to Spain. The people refused to believe it. It was nothing that the king's letter directly stated the fact. It was nothing that official instructions to M. d'Abbadie as to the manner of evacuating and surrendering the province were full and precise. It was nothing that copies of the treaty and of Spain's letter of acceptance were spread out in the council chamber, where the humblest white man could go and read them. Such perfidy was simply incredible. The transfer *must* be a make-believe, or they were doomed to bankruptcy—not figuratively only, but, as we shall presently see, literally also.

So, when doubt could stay no longer, hope took its place—the hope that a prayer to their sovereign might avert the consummation of the treaty, which had already been so inexplicably delayed. On a certain day, therefore, early in 1765, there was an imposing gathering on that Place d'Armes already the place of romantic reminiscences. The voice of the people was to be heard in advocacy of their rights. Nearly all the notables of the town were present ; planters, too, from all the nearer parts of the Delta, with some of the superior council and other officials—an odd motley of lace and flannel, powdered wigs, buckskin, dress-swords, French leather, and cow-hide. One Jean Milhet was there. He was the wealthiest merchant in the town. He had signed the petition of the previous June, with its "features of sedition and insubordination." And he was now sent to France with this new prayer that the king would arrange with Spain to nullify the act of cession.

Milhet, in Paris, sought out Bienville. But the ex-gov-
ernor of the province and unsuccessful campaigner against
its Indian foes, in his eighty-sixth year, was fated to fail
once more in his effort to serve Louisiana. They sought
together the royal audience. But the minister, the Duc
de Choiseul (the transfer had been part of his policy)
adroitly barred the way. They never saw the king, and
their mission was brought to naught with courteous despatch. Such was the word Milhet sent back. But a
hope without foundations is not to be undermined. The
Creoles, in 1766, heard his ill-tidings without despair, and
fed their delusion on his continued stay in France and on
the non-display of the Spanish authority.

By another treaty Great Britain had received, as already
mentioned, a vast territory on the eastern side of the
Mississippi. This transfer was easier to understand. The
English had gone promptly into possession, and, much to
the mental distress of the acting-governor of Louisiana,
M. Aubry (M. d'Abbadie having died in 1765), were making the harbor of New Orleans a highway for their men-
of-war and transports, while without ships, ammunition,
or money, and with only a few soldiers, and they entitled
to their discharge, he awaited Spain's languid receipt of
the gift which had been made her only to keep it from
these very English.

But, at length, Spain moved, or seemed about to move.
Late in the summer a letter came to the superior council
from Havana, addressed to it by Don Antonio de Ulloa, a

commodore in the Spanish navy, a scientific scholar and
author of renown, and now revealed as the royally commissioned governor of Louisiana. This letter announced
that Don Antonio would soon arrive in New Orleans.

Here was another seed of cruel delusion. For month
after month went by, the year closed, January and February, 1766, came and passed, and the new governor had
not made his appearance. Surely, it seemed, this was all
a mere diplomatic manœuver. But, when the delay had
done as much harm as it could, on the 5th of March,
1766, Ulloa landed in New Orleans. He brought with
him only two companies of Spanish infantry, his Government having taken the assurance of France that more
troops would not be needed.

VIII.

THE cession had now only to go into effect. It seemed to the Louisianians a sentence of commercial and industrial annihilation, and it was this belief, not loyalty to France, that furnished the true motive of the Creoles and justification of the struggle of 1768. The merchants were, therefore, its mainspring. But merchants are not apt to be public leaders. They were behind and under the people. Who, then, or what, was in front? An official body whose growth and power in the colony had had great influence in forming the public character of the Creoles —the Superior Council.

It was older than New Orleans. Formed in 1712 of but two members, of whom the governor was one, but gradually enlarged, it dispensed justice and administered civil government over the whole colony, under the ancient "custom of Paris," and the laws, edicts, and ordinances of the kingdom of France. It early contained a germ of popular government in its power to make good the want of a quorum by calling in notable inhabitants of its own selection. By and by its judicial functions had become purely appellate, and it took on features suggestive, at least, of representative rule.

It was this Superior Council which, in 1722, with Bienville at its head, removed to the new settlement of New Orleans, and so made it the colony's capital. In 1723, it was exercising powers of police. It was by this body that, in 1724, was issued that dark enactment which, through the dominations of three successive national powers, remained on the statute-book—the Black Code. One of its articles forbade the freeing of a slave without reason shown to the Council, and by it esteemed good. In 1726, its too free spirit was already receiving the reprimand of the home government. Yet, in 1728, the king assigned to it the supervision of land titles and power to appoint and remove at will a lower court of its own members.

With each important development in the colony it had grown in numbers and powers, and, in 1748, especially, had been given discretionary authority over land titles, such as must have been a virtual control of the whole agricultural community's moral support. About 1752 it is seen resisting the encroachments of the Jesuits, though these were based on a commission from the Bishop of Quebec; and it was this body that, in 1763, boldly dispossessed this same order of its plantations, a year before the home government expelled it from France. In 1758, with Kerlerec at its head, this Council had been too strong for Rochemore, the intendant-commissary, and too free—

jostled him rudely for three years, and then procured of the king his dismissal from office. And lastly, it was this body that d'Abbadie, in another part of the despatch already quoted from, denounced as seditious in spirit, urging the displacement of its Creole members, and the filling of their seats with imported Frenchmen.

Ulloa, the Spanish governor, stepped ashore on the Place d'Armes in a cold rain, with that absence of pomp which characterizes both the sailor and the recluse. The people received him in cold and haughty silence that soon turned to aggression. Foucault, the intendant-commissary, was the first to move. On the very day of the governor's arrival he called his attention to the French paper money left unprovided for in the province. There were seven million livres of it, worth only a fourth of its face value. "What was to be done about it?" The governor answered promptly and kindly : It should be the circulating medium at its market value, pending instructions from Spain. But the people instantly and clamorously took another stand : It must be redeemed at par.

A few days later he was waited on by the merchants. They presented a series of written questions touching their commercial interests. They awaited his answers, they said, in order to know *how to direct their future actions*. In a despatch to his government, Ulloa termed the address " imperious, insolent, and menacing."

The first approach of the Superior Council was quite as offensive. At the head of this body sat Aubry. He was loyal to his king, brave, and determined to execute the orders he held to transfer the province. The troops were under his command. But, by the rules of the Council it was the intendant, Foucault, the evil genius of the hour, who performed the functions of president. Foucault ruled the insurgent Council and signed its pronunciamientos, while Aubry, the sternly protesting but helpless governor, filled the seat of honor. And here, too, sat Lafrénière, the attorney-general. It was he who had harangued the notables and the people on the Place d'Armes when they sent Milhet to France. The petition to the king was from his turgid pen. He was a Creole, the son of a poor Canadian, and a striking type of the people that now looked to him as their leader : of commanding mien, luxurious in his tastes, passionate, overbearing, ambitious, replete with wild energy, and equipped with the wordy eloquence that moves the ignorant or half-informed. The Council requested Ulloa to exhibit his commission. He replied coldly that he would not take possession of the colony until the arrival of additional Spanish troops, which he was expecting ; and that then his dealings would be with the French governor, Aubry, and not with a subordinate civil body.

Thus the populace, the merchants, and the civil government—which included the judiciary—ranged themselves at once in hostility to Spain. The military soon moved forward and took their stand on the same line, refusing point-blank to pass into the Spanish service. Aubry alone recognized the cession and Ulloa's powers, and to him alone Ulloa showed his commission. Yet the Spanish governor virtually assumed control, set his few Spanish soldiers to building and garrisoning new forts at important points in various quarters, and, with Aubry, endeavored to maintain a conciliatory policy pending the arrival of troops. It was a policy wise only because momentarily imperative in dealing with such a people. They were but partly conscious of their rights, but they were smarting under a lively knowledge of their wrongs, and their impatient temper could brook any other treatment with better dignity and less resentment than that which trifled with their feelings.

Ill-will began, before long, to find open utterance. An arrangement by which the three or four companies of French soldiers remained in service under Spanish pay, but under French colors and Aubry's command, was fiercely denounced.

Ulloa was a man of great amiability and enlightenment, but nervous and sensitive. Not only was the defective civilization around him discordant to his gentle tastes, but the extreme contrast which his personal character offered was an intolerable offence to the people. Yet he easily recognized that behind and beneath all their frivolous criticisms and imperious demands, and the fierce determination of their Superior Council to resist all contractions of its powers, the true object of dread and aversion was the iron tyrannies and extortions of Spanish

colonial revenue laws. This feeling it was that had produced the offensive memorial of the merchants; and yet
he met it kindly, and, only two months after his arrival,
began a series of concessions looking to the preservation
of trade with France and the French West Indies, which
the colonists had believed themselves doomed to lose.
The people met these concessions with resentful remon-
strance.   One of the governor's proposals was to fix a
schedule of reasonable prices on all imported goods,
through the appraisement of a board of disinterested citizens.   Certainly it was unjust and oppressive, as any
Spanish commercial ordinance was likely to be; but it
was intended to benefit the mass of consumers. But consumers and suppliers for once had struck hands, and the
whole people raised a united voice of such grievous complaint that the ordinance was verbally revoked.

A further motive—the fear of displacement—moved
the office-holders, and kept them maliciously diligent.
Every harmless incident, every trivial mistake, was
caught up vindictively. The governor's "manner of living, his tastes, his habits, his conversation, the most trivial occurrences of his household," were construed offensively. He grew incensed and began to threaten. In
December, 1767, Jean Milhet returned from France. His
final word of ill-success was only fuel to the fire. The
year passed away, and nine months of 1768 followed.

Ulloa and Aubry kept well together, though Aubry
thought ill of the Spaniard's administrative powers. In

their own eyes they seemed to be having some success. They were, wrote Aubry, "gradually molding Frenchmen to Spanish domination." The Spanish flag floated over the new military posts, the French ensign over the old, and the colony seemed to be dwelling in peace under both standards.

But Ulloa and the Creoles were sadly apart. Repeated innovations in matters of commerce and police were only so many painful surprises to them. They were embarrassed. They were distressed. What was to become of their seven million livres of paper money no one yet could tell. Even the debts that the Spaniards had assumed were unpaid. Values had shrunk sixty-six per cent. There was a specie famine. Insolvency was showing itself on every hand; and the disasters that were to follow the complete establishment of Spanish power were not known but might be guessed. They returned the governor distrust for distrust, censure for censure, and scorn for scorn.

And now there came rumor of a royal decree suppressing the town's commerce with France and the West Indies. It was enough. The people of New Orleans and its adjacent river "coasts," resolved to expel the Spaniards.

IX.

THE INSURRECTION.

NEW ORLEANS, in 1768, was still a town of some thirty-two hundred persons only, a third of whom were black slaves. It had lain for thirty-five years in the reeds and willows with scarcely a notable change to relieve the poverty of its aspect. During the Indian wars barracks had risen on either side of the Place d'Armes. When, in 1758, the French evacuated Fort Duquesne and floated down the Ohio and Mississippi to New Orleans, Kerlerec added other barracks, part of whose ruin still stands in the neighborhood of Barracks Street. Salients had been made at the corners of its palisade wall; there was "a banquette within and a very trifling ditch without." Just beyond this wall, on a part of the land of the banished Jesuits, in a large, deeply shaded garden, was a house that had become the rendezvous of a conspiracy.

Lafrénière sat at the head of its board. His majestic airs had got him the nickname of "Louis Quatorze." Foucault was conspicuous. His friendship with Madame Pradal, the lady of the house, was what is called notor-

ious. Jean Milhet and a brother, Joseph Milhet, and
other leading merchants, Caresse, Petit, and Poupet, were
present; also Doucet, a prominent lawyer, and Marquis, a
captain of Swiss troops; with Balthasar de Masan, Hardy
de Boisblanc, and Joseph Villeré, planters and public
men, the last, especially, a man of weight. And, as if
the name of the city's founder must be linked with all
patriotic disaster, among the number were two of Bienville's nephews—Noyan, a young ex-captain of cavalry,
and Bienville, a naval lieutenant, Noyan's still younger
brother.

On the 25th of October, 1768, the mine was sprung.
From twenty to sixty miles above New Orleans, on the
banks of the Mississippi, lies the Côte des Allemands, the
German coast, originally colonized by John Law's Alsatians.   Here the conspirators had spread the belief that
the Spanish obligations due the farmers there would not
be paid ; and when, on the date mentioned, Ulloa sent an
agent to pay them, he was arrested by a body of citizens
under orders from Villeré, and deprived of the money.

Just beyond the German coast lay the coast of the
" Acadians."   From time to time, since the peace with
England, bands of these exiles from distant Nova Scotia
had found their way to Louisiana, some by way of the
American colonies and the Ohio River, and some—many,
indeed—by way of St. Domingo, and had settled on the
shores of the Mississippi above and below the mouth of La
Fourche and down the banks of that bayou.   Hardships
5

and afflictions had come to be the salt of their bread, and now a last hope of ending their days under the flag for which they had so pathetic an affection depended upon the success of this uprising. They joined the insurgents.

On the 27th, Foucault called a meeting of the Superior Council for the 28th. In the night, the guns at Tchoupitoulas gate—at the upper river corner—were spiked. Farther away, along a narrow road, with the wide and silent Mississippi now hidden by intervening brakes of cotton-wood or willow and now broadening out to view, but always on the right, and the dark, wet, moss-draped forest always on the left, in rude garb and with rude weapons—muskets, fowling pieces, anything—the Germans and Acadians were marching upon the town.

On the morning of the 28th, they entered Tchoupitoulas gate. At the head of the Acadians was Noyan. Villeré led the Germans. Other gates were forced, other companies entered, stores and dwellings were closed, and the insurgents paraded the streets. "All," says Aubry, "was in a state of combustion." The people gathered on the square. "Louis Quatorze" harangued them. So did Doucet and the brothers Milhet. Six hundred persons signed a petition to the Superior Council, asking the official action which the members of that body, then sitting, were ready and waiting to give.

Aubry had a total force of one hundred and ten men. What he could do he did. He sent for Lafrénière, and afterward for Foucault, and protested bitterly, but in vain.

Under his protection, Ulloa retired with his family on board the Spanish frigate, which had slipped her cables from the shore and anchored out in the river. The Spanish governor's staff remained in his house, which they had barricaded, surrounded by an angry mob that filled the air with huzzas for the King of France. The Council met again on the 29th. A French flag had been hoisted in the Place d'Armes, and a thousand insurgents gathered around it demanding the action of the Council. As that body was about to proceed to its final measure, Aubry appeared before it, warning and reproaching its members. Two or three alone wavered, but Lafrénière's counsel prevailed, and a report was adopted enjoining Ulloa to "leave the colony in the frigate in which he came, without delay."

Aubry was invited by the conspirators to resume the government. His response was to charge them with rebellion and predict their ruin. Ulloa, the kindest if not the wisest well-wisher of Louisiana that had held the gubernatorial commission since Bienville, sailed, not in the Spanish frigate, which remained "for repairs," but in a French vessel, enduring at the last moment the songs and jeers of a throng of night roysterers, and the menacing presence of sergeants and bailiffs of the Council.

X.

THE PRICE OF HALF-CONVICTIONS.

THE next move on the part of all concerned was to
hurry forward messengers, with declarations, to the
courts of France and Spain. The colonists sent theirs;
Aubry and Ulloa, each, his; and Foucault, his—a paper
characterized by a shameless double-dealing which leaves
the intendant-commissary alone, of all the participants in
these events, an infamous memory.

The memorial of the people was an absurd confusion of
truth and misstatement. It made admissions fatal to its
pleadings. It made arrogant announcements of unap-
plied principles. It enumerated real wrongs, for which
France and Spain, but not Ulloa, were to blame. And
with these it mingled such charges against the banished
governor as: That he had a chapel in his own house;
that he absented himself from the French churches; that
he enclosed a fourth of the public common to pasture his
private horses; that he sent to Havana for a wet-nurse;
that he ordered the abandonment of a brick-yard near the
town, on account of its pools of putrid water; that he removed leprous children from the town to the inhospitable

settlements at the mouth of the river ; that he forbade
the public whipping of slaves in the town ; that masters
had to go six miles to get a negro flogged ; that he had
landed in New Orleans during a thunder-and-rain storm,
and under other ill omens ; that he claimed to be king of
the colony ; that he offended the people with evidences of
sordid avarice ; and that he added to these crimes—as the
text has it—" many others, equally just [!] and terrible ! "

Not less unhappy were the adulations offered the king,
who so justly deserved their detestation. The conspirators had at first entertained the bold idea of declaring the
colony's independence and setting up a republic. To this
end Noyan and his brother Bienville, about three months
before the outbreak, had gone secretly to Governor El-
liott, at Pensacola, to treat for the aid of British troops.
In this they failed ; and, though their lofty resolution,
which, by wiser leaders, among a people of higher discipline or under a greater faith in the strength of a just
cause, might have been communicated to the popular will,
was not abandoned, it was hidden, and finally suffocated
under a pretence of the most ancient and servile loyalty :
" Great king, the best of kings [Louis XV.], father and
protector of your subjects, deign, sire, to receive into your
royal and fraternal bosom the children who have no other
desire than to die your subjects," etc.

The bearers of this address were Le Sassier, St. Lette,
and Milhet. They appeared before the Duc de Choiseul
unsupported ; for the aged Bienville was dead. St. Lette,

chosen because he had once been an intimate of the duke, was cordially received. But the deputation as a body met only frowns and the intelligence that the King of Spain, earlier informed, was taking steps for a permanent occupation of the refractory province. St. Lette remained in the duke's bosom. Milhet and Le Sassier returned, carrying with them only the cold comfort of an order refunding the colonial debt at three-fifths of its nominal value, in five per cent. bonds.

It was the fate of the Creoles—possibly a climatic result—to be slack-handed and dilatory. Month after month followed the October uprising without one of those incidents that would have succeeded in the history of an earnest people. In March, 1769, Foucault covertly deserted his associates, and denounced them, by letter, to the French cabinet. In April the Spanish frigate sailed from New Orleans. Three intrepid men (Loyola, Gayarre, and Navarro), the governmental staff which Ulloa had left in the province, still remained, unmolested. Not a fort was taken, though it is probable not one could have withstood assault. Not a spade was struck into the ground, or an obstruction planted, at any strategic point, throughout that whole "Creole" spring time which stretches in its exuberant perfection from January to June.

At length the project of forming a republic was revived and was given definite shape and advocacy. But priceless time had been thrown away, the opportune moment had passed, an overwhelming Spanish army and fleet was approaching, and the spirit of the people was paralyzed. The revolt against the injustice and oppression of two royal powers at once, by " the first European colony that entertained the idea of proclaiming her independence," was virtually at an end.

It was the misfortune of the Creoles to be wanting in habits of mature thought and of self-control. They had not made that study of reciprocal justice and natural rights which becomes men who would resist tyranny. They lacked the steady purpose bred of daily toil. With these qualities, the insurrection of 1768 might have been a revolution for the overthrow of French and Spanish misrule and the establishment and maintenance of the right of self-government.

The Creoles were valorous but unreflecting. They had the spirit of freedom, but not the profound principles of right which it becomes the duty of revolutionists to assert and struggle for. They arose fiercely against a confusion of real and fancied grievances, sought to be ungoverned rather than self-governed, and, following distempered leaders, became a warning in their many-sided short-sightedness, and an example only in their audacious courage.

They had now only to pay the penalties ; and it was by an entire inversion of all their first intentions that they at length joined in the struggle which brought to a vigorous birth that American nation of which they finally became a part.

XI.

COUNT O'REILLY AND SPANISH LAWS.

ONE morning toward the end of July, 1769, the people of New Orleans were brought suddenly to their feet by the news that the Spaniards were at the mouth of the river in overwhelming force. There was no longer any room to postpone choice of action.

Marquis, the Swiss captain, with a white cockade in his hat (he had been the leading advocate for a republic), and Petit, with a pistol in either hand, came out upon the ragged, sunburnt grass of the Place d'Armes and called upon the people to defend their liberties. About a hundred men joined them; but the town was struck motionless with dismay; the few who had gathered soon disappeared, and by the next day the resolution of the leaders was distinctly taken, to submit. But no one fled.

On the second morning Aubry called the people to the Place d'Armes, promised the clemency of the illustrious Irishman who commanded the approaching expedition, and sent them away, commanding them to keep within their homes.

Lafrénière, Marquis, and Milhet descended the river,

appeared before the commander of the Spaniards, and by the mouth of Lafrénière in a submissive but brave and manly address presented the homage of the people. The captain-general in his reply let fall the word seditious. Marquis boldly but respectfully objected. He was answered with gracious dignity and the assurance of ultimate justice, and the insurgent leaders returned to New Orleans and to their homes.

The Spanish fleet numbered twenty-four sail. For more than three weeks it slowly pushed its way around the bends of the Mississippi, and on the 18th of August it finally furled its canvas before the town. Aubry drew up his French troops with the colonial militia at the bottom of the Place d'Armes, a gun was fired from the flagship of the fleet, and Don Alexandro O'Reilly, accompanied by twenty-six hundred chosen Spanish troops, and with fifty pieces of artillery, landed in unprecedented pomp, and took formal possession of the province.

On the 21st, twelve of the principal insurrectionists were arrested. Two days later Foucault was also made a prisoner. One other, Braud, the printer of the seditious documents, was apprehended, and a proclamation announced that no other arrests would be made. Foucault, pleading his official capacity, was taken to France, tried by his government, and thrown into the Bastile. Braud pleaded his obligation as government printer to print all public documents, and was set at liberty. Villeré either "died raving mad on the day of his arrest," as stated in the Spanish official report, or met his end in the act of resisting the guard on board the frigate where he had been placed in confinement. Lafrénière, Noyan, Caresse, Marquis, and Joseph Milhet were condemned to be hanged. The supplications both of colonists and Spanish officials saved them only from the gallows, and they fell before the fire of a file of Spanish grenadiers.

The volley made at least one young bride at once an orphan and a widow. For the youthful De Noyan had been newly wed to the daughter of Lafrénière. Judge Gayarre, in his history of Louisiana, tells, as a tradition, that the young chevalier, in prison awaiting execution, being told that his attempt to escape would be winked at by the cruel captain-general, replied that he would live or die with his associates, and so met his untimely end.

Against his young brother, Bienville, no action seems to have been taken beyond the sequestration of his property. He assumed the title of his unfortunate brother, and as the Chevalier de Noyan and lieutenant of a ship of the line, died at St. Domingo nine years after. But Petit, Masan, Doucet, Boisblanc, Jean Milhet, and Poupet were consigned to the Morro Castle, Havana, where they remained a year, and were then set at liberty, but were forbidden to return to Louisiana and were deprived of their property. About the same time Foucault was released from the Bastile. The declaration of the Superior Council was burned on the same Place d'Armes that had

seen it first proclaimed.   Aubry refused a high commission in the Spanish army, departed for France, and had
already entered the River Garonne, when he was ship-
wrecked and lost.   "Cruel O'Reilly"—the captain-general was justly named.

" Cruel O'Reilly."   (From a miniature in possession of Hon. Charles Gayarre, of Louisiana.)

There could, of course, be but one fate for the Superior
Council as an official body, and the Count O'Reilly,
armed with plenary powers, swept it out of existence.
The *cabildo* took its place. This change from French
rule to Spanish lay not principally in the laws, but in the
redistribution of power.   The crown, the sword, and the

cross absorbed the lion's share, leaving but a morsel to be doled out, with much form and pomp, to the *cabildo*. Very quaint and redolent with Spanish romance was this body, which for the third part of a century ruled the pettier destinies of the Louisiana Creoles. Therein sat the six *regidors*, or rulers, whose seats, bought at first at auction, were sold from successor to successor, the crown always coming in for its share of the price. Five of them were loaded down with ponderous titles; the *alferez real* or royal standard bearer; the *alcalde-mayor-provincial*, who overtook and tried offenders escaped beyond town limits; the *alguazil-mayor*, with his eye on police and prisons; the *depositario-general*, who kept and dispensed the public stores; and the *recibidor de penas de cámara*, the receiver of fines and penalties. Above these six sat four whom the six, annually passing out of office, elected to sit over their six successors. These four must be residents and householders of New Orleans. No officer or attaché of the financial department of the realm, nor any bondsman of such, nor any one aged under twenty-six, nor any new convert to the Catholic faith, could qualify. Two were *alcaldes ordinarios*, common judges. In addition to other duties, they held petty courts at evening in their own dwellings, and gave unwritten decisions; but the soldier and the priest were beyond their jurisdiction. A third was *sindico-procurador-general*, and sued for town revenues; and the fourth was town treasurer, the *mayor-domo-de-proprios*. At the bottom of the scale was the *escribano*, or secretary, and at the top, the governor.

It was like a crane,—all feathers. A sample of its powers was its right to sell and revoke at will the meat monopoly and the many other petty municipal privileges which characterized the Spanish rule and have been handed down to the present day in the city's offensive license system. The underlying design of the cabildo's creation seems to have been not to confer, but to scatter and neutralize power in the hands of royal sub-officials and this body. Loaded with titles and fettered with minute ministerial duties, it was, so to speak, the Superior Council shorn of its locks; or if not, then, at least, a body whose members recognized their standing as *guardians* of the people and *servants* of the king.

O'Reilly had come to set up a government, but not to remain and govern. On organizing the cabildo, he announced the appointment of Don Louis de Unzaga, colonel of the regiment of Havana, as governor of the province, and yielded him the chair. But under his own higher commission of captain-general he continued for a time in control. He had established in force the laws of Castile and the Indies and the use of the Spanish tongue in the courts and the public offices. Those who examine the dusty notarial records of that day find the baptismal names, of French and Anglo-Saxon origin, changed to a Spanish orthography, and the indices made upon these instead of upon the surnames.

So, if laws and government could have done it, Louisiana would have been made Spanish. But the change in the laws was not violent. There was a tone of severity and a feature of arbitrary surveillance in those of Spain; but the principles of the French and Spanish systems had a common origin. One remotely, the other almost directly, was from the Roman Code, and they were pointedly similar in the matters which seemed, to the Creole, of supreme importance,—the marital relation, and inheritance. But it was not long before he found that now under the Spaniard, as, earlier, under the French, the laws themselves, and their administration, pointed in very different directions. Spanish *rule* in Louisiana was better, at least, than French, which, it is true, scarcely deserved the name of government. As to the laws themselves, it is worthy of notice that Louisiana " is at this time the only State, of the vast territories acquired from France, Spain, and Mexico, in which the civil law has been retained, and forms a large portion of its jurisprudence."

On the 29th of October, 1770, O'Reilly sailed from New Orleans with most of his troops, leaving the Spanish power entirely and peacefully established. The force left by him in the colony amounted to one thousand two hundred men. He had dealt a sudden and terrible blow; but he had followed it only with velvet strokes. His suggestions to the home government of commercial measures advantageous to New Orleans and the colony, were many, and his departure was the signal for the commencement of active measures intended to induce, if possible, a change in the sentiments of the people,—one consonant with the political changes he had forced upon them.   Such was the kindlier task of the wise and mild Unzaga.

XII.

CROZAT—Law—Louis XV.—Charles III.—whoever at one time or another was the transatlantic master of Louisiana managed its affairs on the same bad principle: To none of them had a colony any inherent rights. They entered into possession as cattle are let into a pasture or break into a field. It was simply a commercial venture projected in the interests of the sovereign's or monopolist's revenues, and restrictions were laid or indulgences bestowed upon it merely as those interests seemed to require. And so the Mississippi Delta, until better ideas could prevail, could not show other than a gaunt, ill-nourished civilization. The weight of oppression, if the governors and other officers on the spot had not evaded the letter of the royal decrees and taught the Creoles to do the same, would actually have crushed the life out of the province.

The merchants of New Orleans, when Unzaga took the governor's chair, dared not import from France anything but what the customs authorities chose to consider articles of necessity. With St. Domingo and Martinique they could only exchange lumber and grain for breadstuffs and wine. Their ships must be passported; their bills of lading were offensively policed; and these "privileges" were only to last until Spain could supplant them by a commerce exclusively her own. They were completely shut out from every other market in the world except certain specified ports of Spain, where, they complained, they could not sell their produce to advantage nor buy what was wanted in the province. They could employ only Spanish bottoms commanded by subjects of Spain; these could not put into even a Spanish-American intermediate port except in distress, and then only under onerous restrictions. They were virtually throttled merely by a rigid application of the theory which had always oppressed them, and only by the loose and flexible administration of which the colony and town had survived and grown, while Anthony Crozat had become bankrupt, Law's Compagnie d'Occident had been driven to other fields of enterprise, and Louis XV. had heaped up a loss of millions more than he could pay.

Ulloa's banishment left a gate wide open which a kind of cattle not of the Spanish brand lost no time in entering.

"I found the English," wrote O'Reilly, in October, 1769, "in complete possession of the commerce of the colony. They had in this town their merchants and traders, with open stores and shops, and I can safely assert that they pocketed nine-tenths of the money spent

6

here. . . . I drove off all the English traders and
the other individuals of that nation whom I found in this
town, and I shall admit here none of their vessels." But
he recommended what may have seemed to him a liberal
measure,—an entirely free trade with Spain and Havana,
and named the wants of the people: "flour, wine, oil,
iron instruments, arms, ammunition, and every sort of
manufactured goods for clothing and other domestic purposes," for which they could pay in "timber, indigo, cotton, furs, and a small quantity of corn and rice."

Unzaga, a man of advanced years and a Spaniard of
the indulgent type, when in 1770 he assumed control, saw
the colony's extremity, and began at once the old policy
of meeting desirable ends by lamentable expedients. His
method was double-acting. He procured, on the one
hand, repeated concessions and indulgences from the
king, while on the other he overlooked the evasion by the
people of such burdens as the government had not lifted.
The Creoles on the plantations took advantage of this
state of affairs. Under cover of trading with the British
posts on the eastern bank of the Mississippi above Orleans
Island, the English traders returned and began again to
supply the Creole planters with goods and slaves. Business became brisk, for anything offered in exchange was
acceptable, revenue laws were mentioned only in jest,
profits were large, and credit was free and long. Against
the river bank, where now stands the suburb of Gretna,
lay moored (when they were not trading up and down the

shores of the stream) two large floating warehouses, fitted up with counters and shelves and stocked with assorted merchandise. The merchants, shut out from these contraband benefits, complained loudly to Unzaga. But they complained in vain. The trade went on, the planters prospered ; the merchants gave them crop-advances, and they turned about and, ignoring their debt, broadened their lands and bought additional slaves from the British traders. Hereupon Unzaga moved, and drawing upon his large reserve of absolute power, gently but firmly checked this imposition.

The governor's quiet rule worked another benefit. While the town was languishing under the infliction of so-called concessions that were so narrowed by provisos as to be almost neutralized, a new oppression showed itself. The newly imported Spanish Capuchins opened such a crusade, not only against their French brethren, but also against certain customs which these had long allowed among the laity, that but for Unzaga's pacific intervention an exodus would have followed which he feared might even have destroyed the colony.

The province could not bear two, and there had already been one. Under O'Reilly so many merchants and mechanics had gone to St. Domingo that just before he left he had ceased to grant passports. Their places were not filled, and in 1773 Unzaga wrote to the Bishop of Cuba that, " There were not in New Orleans and its environs two thousand souls (possibly meaning whites) of all pro-

fessions and conditions," and that most of these were extremely poor.

But conciliation soon began to take effect. Commis-
sions were eagerly taken in the governor's " regiment of
Louisiana," where the pay was large and the sword was
the true emblem of power, and the offices of *regidor* and
alcalde were by-and-by occupied by the bearers of such
ancient Creole names as St. Denis, La Chaise, Fleurieu,
Forstall, Duplessis, Bienvenue, Dufossat, and Livaudais.

In 1776, Unzaga was made captain-general of Carácas,
and the following year, left in charge of Don Bernardo
de Galvez, then about twenty-one years of age, a people
still French in feeling, it is true, yet reconciled in a
measure to Spanish rule.

XIII.

NOW, at length, the Creole and the Anglo-American were to come into active relation to each other—a relation which, from that day to the present, has qualified every public question in Louisiana.

At a happy moment the governorship of Unzaga, a man advanced in life, of impaired vision and failing health, who was begging to be put on the retired list, gave place to the virile administration of one of the most brilliant characters to be seen in the history of the Southwestern United States. Galvez was the son of the Viceroy of Mexico and nephew of the Spanish secretary of state, who was also president of the council of the Indies. He was barely grown to manhood, but he was ardent, engaging, brave, fond of achievement and display, and, withal, talented and sagacious. Says one who fought under him, "He was distinguished for the affability of his manners, the sweetness of his temper, the frankness of his character, the kindness of his heart, and his love of justice."

A change now took place, following the drift of affairs in Europe. The French, instead of the English, mer-

chants, commanded the trade of the Mississippi. The
British traders found themselves suddenly treated with
great rigor. Eleven of their ships, richly laden, were
seized by the new governor, while he exceeded the letter
of the Franco-Spanish treaty in bestowing privileges upon
the French. New liberties gave fresh value to the trade
with French and Spanish-American ports. Slaves were
not allowed to be brought thence, owing to their insurrectionary spirit; but their importation direct from Guinea
was now specially encouraged, and presently the prohibition against those of the West Indies was removed.

Galvez was, as yet, only governor *ad interim;* yet, by
his own proclamation, he gave the colonists the right to
trade with France, and, a few days later, included the
ports of the thirteen British colonies then waging that
war in which the future of the Creoles was so profound-
ly, though obscurely, involved. New liberties were also
given to traders with Spain; the government became the
buyer of the tobacco crop, and a French and French-West
Indian immigration was encouraged.

But these privileges were darkly overshadowed by the
clouds of war. The English issued letters of marque
against Spanish commerce, and the French took open
part in the American revolution. The young governor
was looking to his defences, building gun-boats, and
awaiting from his king the word which would enable him
to test his military talents.

Out of these very conditions, so disappointing in one

direction, sprang a new trade, of the greatest possible
significance in the history of the people. Some eight
years before, at the moment when the arrival of two
thousand six hundred Spanish troops and the non-appear-
ance of their supply-ships had driven the price of provisions in New Orleans almost to famine rates, a brig
entered port, from Baltimore, loaded with flour. The
owner of the cargo was one Oliver Pollock. He offered
to sell it to O'Reilly on the captain-general's own terms,
and finally disposed of it to him at fifteen dollars a bar-
rel, two-thirds the current price. O'Reilly rewarded his
liberality with a grant of free trade to Louisiana for his
life-time. Such was the germ of the commerce of New-
Orleans with the great ports of the Atlantic. In 1776,
Pollock, with a number of other merchants from New
York, Philadelphia, and Boston, who had established
themselves in New Orleans, had begun, with the countenance of Galvez, to supply, by fleets of large canoes, arms
and ammunition to the American agents at Fort Pitt
(Pittsburg). This was repeated in 1777, and, in 1778,
Pollock became the avowed agent of the American Government.

Here, then, was a great turning-point. Immigration
became Anglo-Saxon, a valuable increase of population
taking place by an inflow from the Floridas and the
United States, that settled in the town itself and took the
oath of allegiance to Spain. The commercial acquaintance made a few years before with the Atlantic ports was

now extended to the growing West, and to be cut off from European sources of supply was no longer a calamity, but a lesson of that frugality and self-help in the domestic life which are the secret of public wealth. Between St. Louis and New Orleans, Natchitoches and Natchez (Fort Panmure), there was sufficient diversity of products and industries to complete the circuit of an internal commerce; the Attakapas and Opelousas prairies had been settled by Acadian herdsmen; in 1778, immigrants from the Canary Islands had founded the settlement of Venezuela on La Fourche, Galveztown on the Amite, and that of Terre aux Bœufs just below New Orleans. A paper currency supplied the sometimes urgent call for a circulating medium, and the colonial treasury warrants, or *liberanzas*, were redeemed by receipts of specie from Vera Cruz often enough to keep them afloat at a moderately fair market value.

Were the Creoles satisfied? This question was now to be practically tested. For in the summer of 1779 Spain declared war against Great Britain. Galvez discovered that the British were planning the surprise of New Orleans. Under cover of preparations for defence he made haste to take the offensive. Only four days before the time when he had appointed to move, a hurricane struck the town, demolishing many houses, ruining crops and dwellings up and down the river "coast," and sinking his gun flotilla. Nothing dismayed, the young commander called the people to their old rallying ground on the

Place d'Armes, and with a newly received commission in one hand confirming him as governor, and his drawn sword in the other, demanded of them to answer his challenge: "Should he appear before the cabildo as that commission required, and take the oath of governor? Should he swear to defend Louisiana? Would they stand by him?" The response was enthusiastic. Then, said he, "Let them that love me follow where I lead," and the Creoles flocked around him ready for his behest. Repairing his disasters as best he could, and hastening his ostensibly defensive preparations, he marched, on the 22d of August, 1779, against the British forts on the Mississippi. His force, besides the four Spanish officers who ranked in turn below him, consisted of one hundred and seventy regulars, three hundred and thirty recruits, twenty carbineers, sixty militia men, eighty free men-of-color, six hundred men from the coast ("of every condition and color"), one hundred and sixty Indians, nine American volunteers, and Oliver Pollock. This little army of 1,430 men was without tents or other military furniture, or a single engineer. The gun fleet followed in the river abreast of their line of march, carrying one twenty-four, five eighteen, and four four-pounders. On the 7th of September Fort Bute on Bayou Manchac, with its garrison of twenty men, yielded easily to the first assault of the unsupported Creole militia. The fort of Baton Rouge was found to be very strong, armed with thirteen heavy guns, and garrisoned by five hundred men.

The troops begged to be led to the assault; but Galvez landed his heavy artillery, erected batteries, and on the 21st of September, after an engagement of ten hours, reduced the fort. Its capitulation included the surrender of Fort Panmure, with its garrison of eighty grenadiers, a place that by its position would have been very difficult of assault. The Spanish gun-boats captured in the Mississippi and Manchac four schooners, a brig, and two cutters. On lake Pontchartrain an American schooner fitted out at New Orleans captured an English privateer. A party of fourteen Creoles surprised an English cutter in the narrow waters of Bayou Manchac, and rushing on board after their first fire, and fastening down the hatches, captured the vessel and her crew of seventy men. The Creole militia won the generous praise of their commander for discipline, fortitude and ardor; the Acadians showed an impetuous fury: while the Indians presented the remarkable spectacle of harming no fugitives, and of bearing in their arms to Galvez, uninjured, children who with their mothers had hid themselves in the woods.

In the following February, reënforced from Havana, and commanding the devotion of his Creole militia, Galvez set sail down the Mississippi, with two thousand men, —regulars, Creoles, and free blacks—and issued from that mouth of the river known as the Balize or Pass à l'Outre, intending to attack Fort Charlotte, on the Mobile River. His fleet narrowly escaped total destruction, and his landing on the eastern shore of Mobile River was at-

tended with so much confusion and embarrassment that
for a moment he contemplated a precipitate retreat in the
event of a British advance from Pensacola.   But the
British for some reason were not prompt, and Galvez
pushed forward to Fort Charlotte, erected six batteries,
and engaged the fort, which surrendered on the 14th of
March, to avoid being stormed.   A few days later, the
English arrived from Pensacola in numbers sufficient to
have raised the siege, but with no choice then but to return whence they had come.   Galvez, at that time twenty-
four years of age, was rewarded for this achievement with
the rank of major-general.

He now conceived the project of taking Pensacola.
But this was an enterprise of altogether another magni-
tude.   Failing to secure reënforcements from Havana by
writing for them, he sailed to that place in October, 1780,
to make his application in person, intending, if successful,
to move thence directly upon the enemy.   Delays and
disappointments could not baffle him, and early in March,
1781, he appeared before Pensacola with a ship of the
line, two frigates, and transports containing fourteen hundred soldiers, well furnished with artillery and ammunition.   On the 16th and 17th, such troops as could be
spared from Mobile, and Don Estevan Miró from New
Orleans, with the Louisiana forces, arrived at the western
bank of the Perdido River; and on the afternoon of the
18th, though unsupported by the fleet until dishonor was
staring its jealous commander in the face, Galvez moved

under hot fire, through a passage of great peril, and took up a besieging position.

The investing lines of Galvez and Miró began at once to contract. Early in April, their batteries and those of the fleet opened fire from every side. But the return fire of the English, from a battery erected under their fort, beat off the fleet, and as week after week wore on it began to appear that the siege might be unsuccessful. However, in the early part of May, a shell from the Spaniards having exploded a magazine in one of the English redoubts, the troops from Mobile pressed quickly forward and occupied the ruin, and Galvez was preparing to storm the main fort, when the English raised the white flag. Thus, on the 9th of May, 1781, Pensacola, with a garrison of eight hundred men, and the whole of West Florida, was surrendered to Galvez. Louisiana had heretofore been included under one domination with Cuba ; but now one of the several rewards bestowed upon her governor was the captain-generalship of Louisiana and West Florida. He, however, sailed from St. Domingo to take part in an expedition against the Bahamas, leaving Colonel Miró to govern *ad interim*, and never resumed the governor's chair in Louisiana. In 1785, the captain-generalship of Cuba was given him in addition, and later in the same year, he laid down these offices to succeed his father, at his death, as Viceroy of Mexico. He ruled in this office with great credit, as well as splendor, and died suddenly, in his thirty-eighth year, from the fatigues of a hunt.

Such is a brief summary—too brief for full justice—of the achievements of the Creoles under a gallant Spanish soldier in aid of the war for American independence. Undoubtedly the motive of Spain was more conspicuously and exclusively selfish than the aid furnished by the French; yet a greater credit is due than is popularly accorded to the help afforded in the brilliant exploits of Galvez, discouraged at first by a timid cabildo, but supported initially, finally, and in the beginning mainly, by the Creoles of the Mississippi Delta. The fact is equally true, though much overlooked even in New Orleans, that while Andrew Jackson was yet a child the city of the Creoles had a deliverer from British conquest in Bernardo de Galvez, by whom the way was kept open for the United States to stretch to the Gulf and to the Pacific.

XIV.

IN that city you may go and stand to-day on the spot—still as antique and quaint as the Creole mind and heart which cherish it,—where gathered in 1765 the motley throng of townsmen and planters whose bold repudiation of their barter to the King of Spain we have just reviewed; where in 1768 Lafrénière harangued them, and they, few in number and straitened in purse but not in daring, rallied in arms against Spain's indolent show of authority and drove it into the Gulf. They were the first people in America to make open war distinctly for the expulsion of European rule. But it was not by this episode—it was not in the wearing of the white cockade—that the Creoles were to become an independent republic under British protection, or an American State.

We have seen them in the following year overawed by the heavy hand of Spain, and bowing to her yoke. We have seen them ten years later, under her banner and led by the chivalrous Galvez, at Manchac, at Baton Rouge, at Mobile, and at Pensacola, strike victoriously and " wiser than they knew " for the discomfiture of British power in

America and the promotion of American independence
and unity.   But neither was this to bring them into the
union of free States.   For when the United States became
a nation the Spanish ensign still floated from the flag-staff
in the Plaza de Armas where " Cruel O'Reilly " had hoisted
it, and at whose base the colonial council's declaration of
rights and wrongs had been burned.   There was much more
to pass through, many events and conditions, before the

hand of Louisiana should be unclasped from the hold of
distant powers and placed in that of the American States.

Through all, New Orleans continued to be the key of
the land and river and of all questions concerning them.
A glance around the old square, a walk into any of the
streets that run from it north, east, or south, shows the
dark imprint of the hand that held the town and province
until neither arms, nor guile, nor counterplots, nor bribes,
could hold them back from a destiny that seemed the appointment of nature.

For a while, under Unzaga and Galvez, the frail wooden town of thirty-two hundred souls, that had been the capital under French domination, showed but little change. But 1783 brought peace. It brought also Miró's able administration, new trade, new courage, " forty vessels [in the river] at the same time," and, by 1788, an increase in number to fifty-three hundred. In the same year came the great purger of towns—fire.

Don Vicente José Nuñez, the military treasurer, lived in Chartres Street, near St. Louis, and had a private chapel. On Good Friday, the 21st of March, the wind was very high and from the south, and, either from a falling candle of the altar, or from some other accident or inadvertence, not the first or the worst fire kindled by Spanish piety flared up and began to devour the inflammable town. The people were helpless to stop it. The best of the residences, all the wholesale stores, fell before it. It swept around the north of the plaza, broadening at every step. The town hall, the arsenal, the jail—the inmates of which were barely rescued alive —the parish church, the quarters of the Capuchins, disappeared. In the morning the plaza and the levee were white with tents, and in the smoldering path of the fire, the naked chimneys of eight hundred and fifty-six fallen roofs stood as its monuments. The buildings along the immediate river-front still remained ; but nearly half the town, including its entire central part, lay in ashes.

Old Cabildo as built by Almonaster, 1794, and corner of the Plaza.

Another Spaniard's name stands as the exponent of a miniature renaissance. Don Andreas Almonaster y Roxas was the royal notary and *alferez real*. As far back as 1770 the original government reservations on either side the plaza had been granted the town to be a source of perpetual revenue by ground-rents. Almonaster became their perpetual lessee, the old barracks came down, and two rows of stores, built of brick between wooden pillars, of two and a half stories height, with broad, tiled roofs and dormer windows and bright Spanish awnings, became, and long continued to be the fashionable retail quarter of the town.

Just outside the " Rampart," near St. Peter Street, the hurricane of 1779—Galvez's hurricane, as we may say— had blown down the frail charity hospital which the few thousand livres of Jean Louis, a dying sailor, had founded in 1737. In 1784–86 Almonaster replaced it with a brick edifice costing $114,000. It was the same institution that is now located in Common Street, the pride of the city and State.

In 1787 he built of stuccoed brick, adjoining their convent, the well-remembered, quaint, and homely chapel of the Ursulines. And now, to repair the ravages of fire, he in 1792 began, and in two years completed sufficiently for occupation, the St. Louis Cathedral, on the site of the burned parish church. Louisiana and Florida had just become a bishopric separate from Havana. All these works had been at his own charge. •Later, by contract,

he filled the void made by the burning of the town hall—
which had stood on the south side of the church, facing
the plaza—erecting in its place the hall of the cabildo, the
same that stands there still, made more outlandish, but
not more beautiful, by the addition of a French roof.
The Capuchins, on the other side of the church, had
already replaced their presbytery by the building that
now serves as a court-house. The town erected, on the
river-front just below the plaza, a *halle des boucheries*—
the "old French market." But, except for these two
structures, to the hand of the old *alferez real*, or royal
standard-bearer, belongs the fame of having thrown
together around the most classic spot in the Mississippi
Valley, the most picturesque group of façades, roofs, and
spires in picturesque New Orleans.

But fate made room again for improvement. On the
8th of December, 1794—the wind was this time from the
north—some children, playing in a court in Royale Street,
too near an adjoining hay-store, set fire to the hay. Governor Carondelet—Colonel François Louis Hector, Baron
de Carondelet, a short, plump, choleric Fleming of strong
business qualities, in 1792, when he succeeded Miró, had
provided, as he thought, against this contingency. But,
despite his four *alcaldes de barrio*, with their fire-engines
and firemen and axmen, the fire spread; and in three
hours—for the houses were mere tinder—again burned
out of the heart of the town two hundred and twelve
stores and dwellings. The new buildings at the bottom

"Gratings, balconies, and lime-washed stucco."

of the plaza escaped; but the loss was greater than that of six years before, which was nearly $2,600,000. Only two stores were left standing; the levee and the square again became the camping-ground of hundreds of inhabitants, and the destruction of provisions threatened a famine.

So shingles and thatch and cypress boards had cost enough. From this time the tile roof came into general use. As the town's central parts filled up again, it was with better structures, displaying many Spanish-American features—adobe or brick walls, arcades, inner courts, ponderous doors and windows, heavy iron bolts and gratings (for houses began to be worth breaking into), balconies, portes-cochères, and white and yellow lime-washed stucco, soon stained a hundred colors by sun and rain. Two-story dwellings took the place of one-story, and the general appearance, as well as public safety, was enhanced.

The people were busy, too, in the miry, foul-smelling streets, on the slippery side-walks and on the tree-planted levee. Little by little the home government, at the intercession of the governors—old Unzaga, young Galvez, the suave and energetic Miró—had relaxed its death-grip. A little wooden custom-house, very promptly erected at the upper front corner of the town, had fallen into significant dilapidation, though it was not yet such a sieve but it could catch an export and import duty of six per cent. on all merchandise that did not go round it. The concessions of 1778, neutralized by war and by English blockade, had been revived, enlarged, and extended ten years. Moored against the grassy bank of the brimming river, the black ships were taking in hides and furs, bales of cotton, staves, and skins of indigo for the Spanish market, box-shooks for the West Indian sugar-makers, and tobacco, bought by the Government; and were letting out over their sides machinery and utensils, the red wines of Catalonia, and every product of the manufacturer,—besides negro men and women, girls and boys, for sale singly or in lots on the landing.

On the other side of the town, also, there was, by and by, no little activity. A lake and bayou business was asking room, and a question of sanitation was demanding attention, and in 1794–96 the practical Carondelet gathered a large force of slaves, borrowed from their town and country owners, and dug with pick and shovel in the reeking black soil just beyond the rear fortifications of the town, the "Old Basin" and canal that still bear his name. The canal joined the Bayou St. John, and thus connected ten thousand square yards of artificial harbor with Lake Pontchartrain and the sea-coast beyond. The lands contiguous to this basin and canal were covered with noisome pools, the source of putrid fevers, and, some years later, as Carondelet had urged from the first, the cabildo divided them into garden lots and let them out at low ground-rents to those who would destroy their insalubrity by ditching and draining them into the canal. They began soon to be built on, and have long been en-

The " Old Basin."

tirely settled up ; but their drainage can hardly be considered to have been thorough and final, as, during an inundation eighty years afterward, the present writer passed through its streets in a skiff, with the water as high as the gate-knobs.

By such measures it was that the Spanish king sought " to secure to his vassals the utmost felicity." This was much more than the possession of Louisiana afforded the king. The treaty of peace, signed in 1783 by Great Britain, the United States, France, and Spain, had made the new American power his rival. The western boundary of the States was fixed on the Mississippi from the great lakes to a point nearly opposite the mouth of Red River, and the fortified points along that line, which had fallen so short a time before into the hands of Galvez, were required to be yielded up. Such was the first encroachment of American upon Spanish power in the great basin.

Another influence tending to turn the scales in favor of the States was a change in the agricultural products of the Delta, giving to the commerce of New Orleans a new value for the settlers of the West and the merchants of the Atlantic seaports.

XV.

HOW BORÉ MADE SUGAR.

THE planters of the Delta, on their transfer to Spanish domination, saw indigo, the chief product of
their lands, shut out of market. French protection was
lost and French ports were closed to them. Those of
Spain received them only into ruinous competition with
the better article made in the older and more southern
Spanish colonies. By and by kinder commercial regula-
tions offered a certain relief; but then new drawbacks
began to beset them. Season after season was unfavor-
able, and at length an insect appeared which, by the years
1793–94, was making such ravages that the planters were
in despair. If they could not make indigo they knew not
what to do for a livelihood.

They had tried myrtle-wax and silk, and had long ago
given them up. Everybody made a little tobacco, but the
conditions were not favorable for a large crop in the
Delta. Cotton their grandfathers had known since 1713.
The soil and climate above Orleans Island suited it, and it
had always been raised in moderate quantity. M. Debreuil, a wealthy townsman of New Orleans and a land-

holder, a leading mind among the people, had invented a cotton-gin effective enough to induce a decided increase in the amount of cotton raised in the colony. Yet a still better mode of ginning the staple from the seed was needed to give the product a decided commercial value. There was some anticipation of its possible importance, and certain ones who gave the matter thought had, in 1760, recommended the importation of such apparatus as could be found in India. In 1768 cotton had become an article of export from New Orleans, and in the manifesto with which the insurgents banished Ulloa it is mentioned as a product whose culture, " improved by experience, promised the planter the recompense of his toils."

At the time of the collapse in the indigo production, the Creoles were still experimenting with cotton ; but the fame of Eli Whitney's newly invented cotton-gin had probably not reached them. There must have been few of them, indeed, who supposed that eight years later the cotton crop of Louisiana and export from New Orleans would be respectively 20,000 and 34,000 300-pound bales. They turned for a time in another direction. The lower Delta was a little too far south for cotton as a sure crop. They would try once more, as their fathers had tried, to make merchantable sugar.

On a portion of the city's present wholesale business district, near Tchoupitoulas Street, this great staple had been first planted in Louisiana by the Jesuit fathers in 1751. They had received their seed, or rather layers, from St. Domingo. It had been grown in the town's vicinity ever since, but there only, and in trivial quantity. Nothing more than syrup, if even so much, was made from it until in 1758 M. Debreuil, the same who had experimented with cotton, built a sugar-mill on his plantation—now that part of the third district adjoining the second, on the river-front—and endeavored to turn a large crop of cane into sugar.

Accounts of the result vary. Sugar, it seems, however, was made, and for a time the industry grew. But the sugar was not of a sort to ship to the world's markets; it was poorly granulated and very wet, and for several years was consumed within the province. In 1765 the effort was at length made to export it to France; but half the first cargo leaked out of the packages before the vessel could make port.

Then came the cession to Spain, and with it paralysis. The half-developed industry collapsed. But in 1791 the blacks of St. Domingo rose in rebellion. Refugees flew in every direction. A few found their way to Louisiana. They had been prosperous sugar-makers, and presently the efforts that had ceased for twenty-five years came again to life. Two Spaniards, Mendez and Solis, in that year erected on the confines of New Orleans, the one a distillery and the other a battery of sugar-kettles, and manufactured rum and syrup.

Still the Creoles, every year less able than the year before to make rash experiments, struggled against the misfortunes that multiplied around the cultivation of indigo, until 1794 found them without hope.

At this juncture appeared Etienne de Boré. He was a man of fifty-four, a Creole of the Illinois district, but of a

Etienne de Boré.

distinguished Norman family; he had lived in France from the age of four to thirty-two, had served with the king's *mousquetaires*, had married a lady whose estate was in Louisiana near New Orleans, and returning with her to the province, had become an indigo planter. The year 1794 found him face to face with ruin. His father-in-law, Destréhan, had in former years been one of the last to abandon sugar culture. His wife and friends warned him against the resolution he was taking ; but he persisted in his determination to abandon indigo, and risk all that was left to him on the chance of a success which, if achieved, would insure deliverance and fortune to himself and the community. He bought a quantity of canes from Mendez and Solis, planted on the land where the Seventh District (late Carrollton) now stands, and while his crop was growing erected a mill, and prepared himself for the momentous season of " grinding."

His fellow-planters looked on with the liveliest—not always with the most hopeful—interest, and at length they gathered about him to see the issue of the experiment in which only he could be more deeply concerned than they. In the whole picturesque history of the Louisiana Creoles few scenes offer so striking a subject for the painter as that afforded in this episode : The dark sugar-house ; the battery of huge caldrons, with their yellow juice boiling like a sea, half-hidden in clouds of steam ; the half-clad, shining negroes swinging the gigantic utensils with which the seething flood is dipped from kettle to kettle ; here, grouped at the end of the battery, the Creole planters with anxious faces drawing around their central figure as closely as they can ; and in the midst the old *mousquetaire*, dipping, from time to time, the thickening juice, repeating again and again his simple tests, until, in the moment of final trial, there is a common look of suspense, and instantly after it the hands are dropped, heads are raised, the brow is wiped, and there is a long breath of relief—" it granulates ! "

The people were electrified. Etienne de Boré marketed $12,000 worth of superior sugar. The absence of interdictions that had stifled earlier trade enabled him to sell his product to advantage. The agriculture of the Delta was revolutionized ; and, seven years afterward, New Orleans was the market for 200,000 gallons of rum, 250,000 gallons of molasses, and 5,000,000 pounds of sugar. The town contained some twelve distilleries— probably not a subject for unmixed congratulation—and a sugar refinery which produced about 200,000 pounds of loaf sugar; while on the other hand the production of indigo had declined to a total of 3,000 pounds, and soon after ceased.

8

XVI.

THE CREOLES SING THE MARSEILLAISE.

THE Spanish occupation never became more than a conquest. The Spanish tongue, enforced in the courts and principal public offices, never superseded the French in the mouths of the people, and left but a few words naturalized in the corrupt French of the slaves. To African organs of speech *cocodrie*, from *cocodrilo*, the

crocodile, was easier than *caiman*, the alligator; the terrors of the calaboza, with its chains and whips and branding irons, were condensed into the French tri-syllabic *calaboose;* while the pleasant institution of *ñapa*—the petty gratuity added, by the retailer, to anything bought—grew the pleasanter, drawn out into Gallicized *lagnappe*.

In the Cabildo.

The only newspaper in the town or province, as it was also the first, though published under the auspices of Carondelet, was the "Moniteur de la Louisiane," printed entirely in French. It made its first appearance in 1794.

Spanish Ursulines, sent from Havana to impart their own tongue, had to teach in French instead, and to content themselves with the feeble achievement of extorting the Spanish catechism from girls who recited with tears rolling down their cheeks. The public mind followed— though at a distance—the progress of thought in France. Many Spaniards of rank cast their lot with the Creoles. Unzaga married a Maxent; Galvez, her sister—a woman, it is said, of extraordinary beauty and loveliness; Gayarré wedded Constance de Grandpré ; the intendant Odvardo, her sister ; Miró, a de Macarty. But the Creoles never became Spanish ; and in society balls where the Creole civilian met the Spanish military official, the cotillon was French or Spanish according as one or the other party was the stronger, a question more than once decided by actual onset and bloodshed. The Spanish rule was least unpopular about 1791, when the earlier upheavals of the French revolution were regarded distantly, and before the Republic had arisen to fire the Creole's long-suppressed enthusiasm. Under Galvez, in 1779–82, they rallied heartily around the Spanish colors against their hereditary British foe. But when, in 1793, Spain's foe was republican France, Carondelet found he was only holding a town of the enemy. Then the Creole could no longer restrain himself. "La Marseillaise ! La Marseillaise ! " he cried in his sorry little theatre ; and in the drinking-shops—that were thick as autumn leaves—he sang, defiantly, " *Ça ira, ça ira, les aristocrates à la lanterne*," though there was not a lamp-post in his town until three years later, when the same governor put up eighty.

Meantime Spain's hand came down again with a pressure that brought to mind the cruel past. The people were made to come up and subscribe themselves Spaniards, and sundry persons were arrested and sent to Havana. The baron rebuilt the fortifications on a new and stronger plan. At the lower river corner was Fort St. Charles, a five-sided thing for one hundred and fifty men, with brick-faced parapet eighteen feet thick, a ditch, and a covert way ; at the upper river corner was Fort St. Louis, like it, but smaller. They were armed with about twelve eighteen- and twelve-pounders. Between them, where Toulouse Street opened upon the river-front, a large battery crossed fires with both. In the rear of the town were three lesser forts, mere stockades, with fraises. All around from fort to fort ran a parapet of earth surmounted with palisades, and a moat forty feet wide and seven deep. "These fortifications," wrote Carondelet, "would not only protect the city against the attack of an enemy, but also keep in check its inhabitants. But for them," he said, " a revolution would have taken place."

This was in 1794. The enemy looked for from without was the pioneers of Kentucky, Georgia, etc. The abridgment of their treaty rights on the Mississippi had fretted them. Instigated by Genet, the French minister

to the United States, and headed by one Clark and by
Auguste de la Chaise, a Louisiana Creole of powerful
family, who had gone to Kentucky for the purpose, they
were preparing to make a descent upon New Orleans for
its deliverance; when events that await recital arrested the
movement.

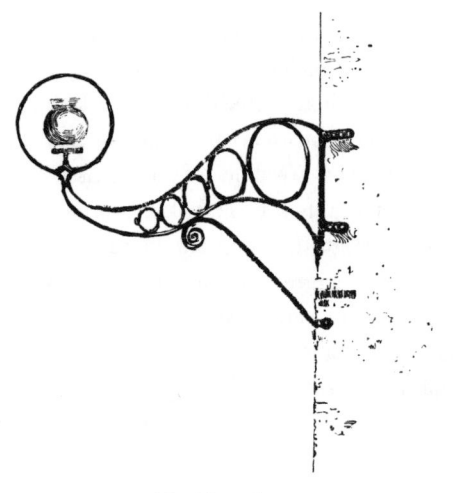

A Royal Street Corner.

XVII.

CARONDELET had strengthened the walls that immured the Creoles of New Orleans; but, outside, the messenger of their better destiny was knocking at the gate with angry impatience. Congress had begun, in 1779, to claim the freedom of the Mississippi. The treaty of 1783 granted this; but in words only, not in fact. Spain intrigued, Congress menaced, and oppressions, concessions, aggressions, deceptions, and corruption lengthened out the years. New Orleans—" Orleens" the Westerners called it—there was the main difficulty. Every one could see now its approaching commercial greatness. To Spain it was the key of her possessions. To the West it was the only possible breathing-hole of its commerce.

Miró was still governing *ad interim*, when, in 1785, there came to him the commissioners from the State of Georgia demanding liberty to extend her boundary to the Mississippi, as granted in the treaty of peace. Miró answered wisely, referring the matter to the governments of America and Spain, and delays and exasperations continued. By 1786, if not earlier, the flat-boat fleets that came floating out of the Ohio and Cumberland, seeking on the lower Mississippi a market and port for their hay and bacon and flour and corn, began to be challenged from the banks, halted, seized, and confiscated. The exasperated Kentuckians openly threatened and even planned to descend in flat-boats full of long rifles instead of breadstuffs, and make an end of controversy by the capture of New Orleans. But milder counsels restrained them, and they appealed to Congress to press Spain for the commercial freedom which they were determined to be deprived of no longer.

Miró, and Navarro, the intendant, did well to be alarmed. They wrote home urging relief through certain measures which they thought imperative if New Orleans, Louisiana, the Floridas, or even Mexico, was to be saved from early conquest. "*No hay que perder tiempo*"—"There is no time to be lost." They had two schemes: one, so to indulge the river commerce that the pioneers swarming down upon their borders might cross them, not as invaders, but as immigrants, yielding allegiance to Spain; the other, to foment a revolt against Congress and the secession of the West. These schemes were set on foot; a large American immigration did set in, and the small town of New Madrid still commemorates the extravagant calculations of Western grantees.

There had lately come to Kentucky a certain man whose ready insight and unscrupulous spirit of intrigue had promptly marked the turn of events. This was General James Wilkinson, of the United States service, a man early distrusted by President Washington, long suspected by the people, and finally tried for treasonable designs and acquitted for want of evidence which the archives of Spain, to which access could not at that time be obtained, have since revealed. This cunning schemer and speculator, in June, 1787, sent and followed to New Orleans a large fleet of flat-boats loaded with the produce of the West, and practising on the political fears of Miró, secured many concessions. By this means he made way for a trade which began at once to be very profitable to New Orleans, not to say to many Spanish officials. But it was not by this means only. At the same time, he entered into a secret plot with Miró and Spain for that disruption of the West from the East which she sought to effect. "The delivering up of Kentucky into his Majesty's hands, which is the main object to which Wilkinson has promised to devote himself entirely," so wrote Miró to the Spanish Secretary of State, January 8, 1788, and Wilkinson's own letters, written originally in cipher, and now in the archives of Spain, reduced to the Spanish tongue, complete the overwhelming evidence. "When this is done, . . . I shall disclose so much of our great scheme," etc. "Be satisfied, nothing shall deter me from attending exclusively to the object we have on hand." "The only feasible plan"—this was a year later —" . . . was . . . separation from the United

States, and an alliance with Spain." Such was the flat-boat toll paid by this lover of money and drink.

But, neither for the Kentuckian nor the Creole was an export trade more than half a commerce. Philadelphia partly supplied the deficiency, though harried by corrupt double-dealings. Miró and Navarro favored and promoted this trade; but Gardoqui, the Spanish minister at Philadelphia, not sharing in the profits, moved vigorously against it, and there was dodging and doubling—all the subterfuges of the contrabandist, not excepting false arrests and false escapes. The fire of 1788 gave Navarro excuse to liberate a number whom fear of the king had forced him to imprison, and to give them back their confiscated goods. Such was one branch of the academy that, in later years, graduated the pirates of Barataria.

The scarcity of provisions after the fire was made to help this Philadelphia trade. Miró sent three vessels to Gardoqui (who was suddenly ready to coöperate) for 3,000 barrels of flour, and such other goods as the general ruin called for. And here entered Wilkinson, and in August, 1788, received through his agent, Daniel Clark, in New Orleans, a cargo of dry goods and other articles for the Kentucky market, probably the first boat-load of manufactured commodities that ever went up the Mississippi to the Ohio. Others followed Wilkinson's footsteps in matters of trade, and many were the devices for doing one thing while seeming to do another. A pretence of coming to buy lands and settle secured passports for their flat-boats and keel-boats, and the privilege of selling and buying free of duty. A profession of returning for families and property opened the way back again up the tortuous river, or along the wild, robber-haunted trails of the interior.

So the Creoles, in their domestic commerce, were striking hands with both the eastern and western "American." As to their transatlantic commerce, the concessions of 1782 had yielded it into the hands of the French, and there it still remained. "France," wrote Miró in 1790, "has the monopoly of the commerce of this colony." It suited him not to mention Philadelphia or the Ohio. But war presently brought another change.

XVIII.

THE port of New Orleans was neither closed nor open.
Spain was again in fear of Great Britain. The
United States minister at Madrid was diligently pointing
to the possibility of a British invasion of Louisiana from
Canada, by way of the Mississippi; to the feebleness of
the Spanish foothold; to the unfulfilled terms of the
treaty of 1783; to the restlessness of the Kentuckians; to
everything, indeed, that could have effect in the effort to
extort the cession of "Orleans" and the Floridas. But
Spain held fast, and Miró, to the end of his governorship,
plotted with Wilkinson and with a growing number of
lesser schemers equally worthy of their country's execra-
tion.

Difficulties were multiplying when, at the close of
1791, Miró gave place to Carondelet. Some were internal; and the interdiction of the slave-trade with re-
volted St. Domingo, the baron's fortifications, the banishment of Yankee clocks branded with the Goddess of
Liberty, etc., were signs of them, not cures. In February,
1793, America finally wormed from Spain a decree of

open commerce, for her colonies, with the United States and Europe. Thereupon Philadelphians began to establish commercial houses in New Orleans.

On the side of the great valley, the Kentuckian was pressing with all the strength of his lean and sinewy shoulder. "Since my taking possession of the government," wrote Carondelet, in 1794, "this province . . . has not ceased to be threatened by the ambitious designs of the Americans." "A nation," as Navarro had earlier called them, "restless, proud, ambitious, and capable of the most daring enterprise." Besides them, there were La Chaise, also, and Genet, and the Jacobins of Philadelphia.

It was to President Washington's vigilance and good faith that the baron owed the deliverance of the province from its dangers; not to his own defences, his rigid police, nor his counter-plots with Thomas Power and others. These dangers past, he revived the obstruction and oppression of the river trade, hoping, so, to separate yet the Western pioneers from the union of States, to which they had now become devoted.

But events tended ever one way, and while Carondelet was still courting Wilkinson through Power, a treaty, signed at Madrid October 20, 1795, declared the Mississippi free to the Americans. New Orleans was made a port of deposit for three years, free of all duty or charge, save "a fair price for the hire of the store-houses." The privilege was renewable at the end of the term, unless

transferred by Spain to some "equivalent establishment"
on the river bank.

Still Carondelet held the east bank of the river, tem-
porizing with the American authorities through his col-
league, General Gayoso de Lemos, the Spanish commissioner, for making the transfer. He spent bribes freely,
and strengthened his fortifications, not against Federal
commanders only, but against the western immigrants
who had crowded into the province, and against the re-
newed probability of invasion from Canada.

He made two other efforts to increase his strength.
At the request of the cabildo he prohibited, for the time,
the further importation of slaves, a plot for a bloody
slave insurrection having been discovered in Pointe
Coupée, a hundred and fifty miles up the Mississippi
from New Orleans, and put down with much killing,
whipping, and hanging. And he received with extravagant hospitality certain noble French refugees, who had
sought asylum from the Reign of Terror on the wild
western border of the United States. They were furnished with transportation from New Madrid to the
Washita, and were there to receive two hundred acres
of land and one hundred dollars in money for every
mechanic or farmer brought by them into the projected
colony. The grant to the Marquis of Maison Rouge
under these conditions was to embrace thirty thousand
acres. That to the Baron de Bastrop was to cover one
hundred and eight square miles, and there were others

of less imperial extent. The royal approval was secured upon these grants, but the grantees never fulfilled the conditions laid upon them, and these great enterprises melted down to famous lawsuits. French *emigrés*, nevertheless, did and had already settled in Louisiana under more reasonable grants got with more modest promises. The town of St. Martinsville, on the Bayou Têche, was settled by them and nicknamed *le petit Paris*—the little Paris; and a chapter might well be devoted to this episode in the history of the Creoles. New Orleans even had the pleasure at length of entertaining for many weeks, with great gayety and social pomp, the Duke of Orleans, afterward King Louis Philippe, and his two brothers, the Duke of Montpensier and the Count of Beaujolais. Boré and the Marquis Marigny de Mandeville were among their entertainers.

The Creoles' republican enthusiasm found vent in a little patriotic singing and shouting, that cost six of them twelve months each of Cuban exile ; otherwise they remained, through all, passive. We have seen how they passed through an agricultural revolution. But they were no more a writing than a reading people, and what tempests of emotion many of them may have concealed while war was being waged against France, while the Gulf was being scoured by French privateers, and when one of these seized, and for eight days held, the mouth of the Mississippi, may only be conjectured. We know that Etienne de Boré escaped arrest and transportation only by

The Marigny House, where Louis Philippe stopped in 1798.

reason of his rank and the people's devotion to him as a public benefactor.

In 1797 Carondelet gave place to Gayoso de Lemos. Wilkinson, who was in chief command of the American forces in the West, grew coy and cold. The encroachments of the double-dealing general's subordinates could be resisted by the Spaniard no longer, and in March, 1798, he abandoned by stealth, rather than surrendered, the territory east of the Mississippi, so long unjustly retained from the States.

All the more did the Creole city remain a bone of contention. On the close of the three-years' term named in the treaty of 1795, the intendant, Morales, a narrow and quarrelsome old man, closed the port, and assigned no other point to take its place.

But the place had become too important, and the States too strong for this to be endured. The West alone could muster twenty thousand fighting men. John Adams was President. Secret preparations were at once set on foot for an expedition against New Orleans in overwhelming force. Boats were built, and troops had already been ordered to the Ohio, when it began to be plain that the President must retire from office at the close of his term, then drawing near; and by and by Spain disavowed her intendant's action and reopened the closed port.

Meanwhile another eye was turned covetously upon Louisiana, and one who never moved slowly was about to hurry her fate to a climax.

9

XIX.

"FRANCE has cut the knot," wrote Minister Livingston to Secretary Madison. It is the word of Bonaparte himself, that his first diplomatic act with Spain had for its object the recovery of Louisiana. His power enabled him easily to outstrip American negotiations, and on the 1st of October, 1800, the Spanish King entered privately into certain agreements by which, on the 21st of March, 1801, Louisiana, vast, but to Spain unremunerative and indefensible, passed secretly into the hands of the First Consul in exchange for the petty Italian "kingdom of Etruria." When Minister Livingston wrote, in November, 1802, the secret was no longer unknown.

On the 26th of March, 1803, M. Laussat, as French Colonial Prefect, landed in New Orleans, specially commissioned to prepare for the expected arrival of General Victor with a large body of troops, destined for the occupation of the province, and to arrange for the establishment of a new form of government. The Creoles were filled with secret consternation. Their fields, and streets,

and dwellings were full of slaves. They had heard the
First Consul's words to the St. Domingans: "Whatever
be your color or your origin, you are free." But their
fears were soon quieted, when Laussat proclaimed the design of their great new ruler to "preserve the empire of
the laws and amend them slowly in the light of experience
only." The planters replied that "their long-cherished
hope was gratified, and their souls filled with the delir-
ium of extreme felicity;" and the townsmen responded:
"Happy are the colonists of Louisiana who have lived
long enough to see their reunion to France, which they
have never ceased to desire, and which now satisfies their
utmost wish."

Governor Gayoso had died of yellow fever in 1799—it
is said shortly after a night's carousal with Wilkinson.
He had been succeeded by the Marquis of Casa Calvo,
and he, in 1801, by a weak, old man, Don Juan Manuel
de Salcedo. The intendant Morales had continued to
hate, dread, and hamper American immigration and commerce, and in October, 1802, had once more shut them
out of New Orleans until six months later again discoun-
tenanced by his king.

In Congress debate narrowed down to the question
whether New Orleans and the Floridas should be bought
or simply swept down upon and taken. But the executive department was already negotiating; and, about the
time of Laussat's landing in Louisiana, Messrs. Livingston
and Monroe were commissioned to treat with France for

a cession of New Orleans and the Floridas, " or as much thereof as the actual proprietor can be prevailed on to part with."

Bonaparte easily saw the larger, but unconfessed wish of the United States. Louisiana, always light to get and heavy to hold, was slipping even from his grasp. He was about to rush into war with the English. " They have," he exclaimed passionately to his ministers, "twenty ships of war in the Gulf of Mexico. . . . I have not a moment to lose in putting it [his new acquisition] out of their reach. They [the American commissioners] only ask of me one town in Louisiana ; but I already consider the colony as entirely lost." And a little later, walking in the garden of St. Cloud, he added to Marbois—whom he trusted rather than Talleyrand—" Well! you have charge of the treasury; let them give you one hundred million francs, pay their own claims, and take the whole country." When the minister said something about the rights of the colonists, "Send your maxims to the London market," retorted the First Consul.

The price finally agreed upon was eighty million francs, out of which the twenty million francs of American citizens' claims due by France were to be paid, and Louisiana was bought. Monsieur Marbois and Messrs. Livingston and Monroe signed the treaty on the 30th of April, 1803. As they finished, they rose and shook hands. " We have lived long," said Livingston, " but this is the noblest work of our lives."

About the last of July, when Casa Calvo and Salcedo, Spanish commissioner and governor, had proclaimed the coming transfer to France, and Laussat, the French prefect, was looking hourly for General Victor and his forces, there came to New Orleans a vessel from Bordeaux with the official announcement that Louisiana had been ceded to the United States.

On the 30th of November, with troops drawn up in line on the Place d'Armes, and with discharges of artillery, Salcedo, fitly typifying, in his infirm old age, the decaying kingdom which he represented, delivered to Laussat, in the hall of the cabildo, the keys of New Orleans ; while Casa Calvo, splendid in accomplishments, titles, and appearance, declared the people of Louisiana absolved from their allegiance to the King of Spain. From the flag-staff in the square the Spanish colors descended, the French took their place, and the domination of Spain in Louisiana was at an end.

On Monday, December the 20th, 1803, with similar ceremonies, Laussat turned the province and the keys of its port over to Commissioners Claiborne and Wilkinson. The French tricolor, which had floated over the Place d'Armes for but twenty days, gave place to the stars and stripes, and New Orleans was an American town.

Within a period of ninety-one years Louisiana had changed hands six times. From the direct authority of Louis XIV. it had been handed over, in 1712, to the commercial dominion of Anthony Crozat. From Crozat it had passed, in 1717, to the Compagnie de l'Occident ; from the company, in 1731, to the undelegated authority of Louis XV. ; from him, in 1762, to Spain ; from Spain,

Autographs from the Archives.

in 1801, back to France ; and at length, in 1803, from France to the United States, finally emancipated from the service and bargainings of European masters.

XX.

NEW ORLEANS had been under the actual sway of the Spaniard for thirty-four years. Ten thousand inhabitants were gathered in and about its walls. Most of the whites were Creoles. Even in the province at large these were three in every four. Immigrants from Malaga, the Canaries, and Nova Scotia had passed on through the town and into the rural districts. Of the thousands of Americans, only a few scores of mercantile pioneers came as far as the town—sometimes with families, but generally without. Free trade with France had brought some French merchants, and the Reign of Terror, as we have seen, had driven here a few royalists. The town had filled and overflowed its original boundaries. From the mast-head of a ship in the harbor one looked down upon a gathering of from twelve hundred to fourteen hundred dwellings and stores, or say four thousand roofs—to such an extent did slavery multiply outhouses. They were of many kinds, covered with half-cylindrical or with flat tiles, with shingles, or with slates, and showed an endless variety in height and in bright confusion of color and form—verandas and balconies, dormer windows, lattices, and belvederes. Under the river bank, "within ten steps of Tchoupitoulas Street," where land has since formed and been covered with brick stores for several squares, the fleets of barges and flatboats from the West moored and unloaded, or retailed their contents at the water's edge. Farther down, immediately abreast of the town, between the upper limits and the Place d'Armes, lay the shipping—twenty or more vessels of from 100 to 200 tons burden, hauled close against the bank. Still farther on, beyond the Government warehouses, was the mooring-place of the vessels of war. Looking down into the streets —Toulouse, St. Peter, Conti, St. Louis, Royale, Chartres —one caught the brisk movements of a commercial port. They were straight, and fairly spacious, for the times; but unpaved, ill-drained, filthy, poorly lighted, and often impassable for the mire.

The town was fast becoming one of the chief seaports of America. Already, in 1802, 158 American merchantmen, 104 Spanish, and 3 French, registering 31,241 tons, had sailed from her harbor, loaded. The incoming tonage for 1803 promised an increase of over 37 per cent. It exported of the products of the province alone over $2,000,000 value. Its imports reached $2,500,000. Thirty-four thousand bales of cotton ; 4,500 hogsheads of sugar ; 800 casks—equivalent to 2,000 barrels—of molasses ; rice, peltries, indigo, lumber, and sundries, to the value of $500,000 ; 50,000 barrels of flour ; 3,000 barrels of beef and pork ; 2,000 hogsheads of tobacco ; and smaller quantities of corn, butter, hams, meal, lard, beans, hides, staves, and cordage, had passed in 1802 across its famous levee.

Everywhere the restless American was conspicuous, and, with the Englishman and the Irishman, composed the majority of the commercial class. The French, except a few, had subsided into the retail trade or the mechanical callings. The Spaniards not in military or civil service were generally humble Catalans, keepers of shops, and of the low cabarets that occupied almost every street corner. The Creole was on every side—handsome, proud, illiterate, elegant in manner, slow, a seeker of office and military commission, ruling society with fierce exclusiveness, looking upon toil as the slave's proper badge, lending money now at twelve and now at twenty-four per cent., and taking but a secondary and unsympa-

thetic part in the commercial life from which was springing the future greatness of his town. What could he do?
The American filled the upper Mississippi Valley. England and the Atlantic States, no longer France and Spain,
took its products and supplied its wants. The Anglo-
Saxon and the Irishman held every advantage; and, ill-
equipped and uncommercial, the Creole was fortunate to
secure even a third or fourth mercantile rank in the city
of his birth. But he had one stronghold. He owned the
urban and suburban real estate, and presently took high
station as the seller of lots and as a *rentier*. The confis
cated plantations of the Jesuits had been, or were being,
laid out in streets. From 1801, when Faubourg St. Mary
contained only five houses, it had grown with great
rapidity.

Other faubourgs were about springing up. The high
roofs of the aristocratic suburb St. Jean could be seen
stretching away among their groves of evergreen along the
Bayou road, and clustering presently into a village near
where a "Bayou bridge" still crosses the stream, some
two hundred yards below the site of the old one. Here
gathered the larger craft of the lake trade, while the
smaller still pushed its way up Carondelet's shoaled and
neglected, yet busy canal.

Outwardly the Creoles of the Delta had become a
graceful, well-knit race, in full keeping with the freedom
of their surroundings. Their complexion lacked ruddiness,
but it was free from the sallowness of the Indies. There

was a much larger proportion of blondes among them than is commonly supposed. Generally their hair was of a chestnut, or but little deeper tint, except that in the city a Spanish tincture now and then asserted itself in black hair and eyes. The women were fair, symmetrical, with pleasing features, lively, expressive eyes, well-rounded throats, and superb hair; vivacious, decorous, exceedingly tasteful in dress, adorning themselves with superior effect in draperies of muslin enriched with embroideries and much garniture of lace, but with a more moderate display of jewels, which indicated a community of limited wealth. They were much superior to the men in quickness of wit, and excelled them in amiability and in many other good qualities. The more pronounced faults of the men were generally those moral provincialisms which travellers recount with undue impatience. They are said to have been coarse, boastful, vain; and they were, also, deficient in energy and application, without well-directed ambition, unskilful in handicraft—doubtless through negligence only —and totally wanting in that community feeling which begets the study of reciprocal rights and obligations, and reveals the individual's advantage in the promotion of the common interest. Hence, the Creoles were fonder of pleasant fictions regarding the salubrity, beauty, good order, and advantages of their town, than of measures to justify their assumptions. With African slavery they were, of course, licentious, and they were always ready for the duelling-ground; yet it need not seem surprising that a people so beset by evil influences from every direction were generally unconscious of a reprehensible state of affairs, and preserved their self-respect and a proud belief in their moral excellence. Easily inflamed, they were as easily discouraged, thrown into confusion, and overpowered, and they expended the best of their energies in trivial pleasures, especially the masque and the dance; yet they were kind parents, affectionate wives, tractable children, and enthusiastic patriots.

Transom in the Pontalba Buildings, Jackson Square.

XXI.

L ITTLE wonder that it is said the Creoles wept as they stood on the Place d'Armes and saw the standard of a people, whose national existence was a mere twenty-years' experiment, taking the place of that tricolor on which perched the glory of a regenerated France. On that very spot some of them had taken part in the armed repudiation of the first cession. The two attitudes and the two events differed alike. The earlier transfer had come loaded with drawbacks and tyrannous exactions; the latter came freighted with long-coveted benefits and with some of the dearest rights of man. This second, therefore, might bring tears of tender regret; it might force the Creole into civil and political fellowship with the detested *Américain;* but it could not rouse the sense of outrage produced by the cession to Spain, or of uniform popular hatred against the young Virginian whom President Jefferson had transferred from the Governorship of the Territory of Mississippi to that of Louisiana. O'Reilly, the Spanish Captain-General, had established a government whose only excellence lay in its strength; Claiborne came

to set up a power whose only strength lay in its excellence. His task was difficult mainly because it was to be
done among a people distempered by the badness of earlier
rule, and diligently wrought upon by intriguing Frenchmen
and Spanish officials. His wisest measures, equally with his
broadest mistakes, were wordily resented. His ignorance

William Charles Cole Claiborne, Governor of Louisiana from 1803 to 1816.

of the French language, his large official powers, Wilkinson's bad habits, a scarcity of money, the introduction of
the English tongue, and of a just proportion of American
appointees into the new courts and public offices, the use
of bayonets to suppress disorder at public balls, a supposed partiality for Americans in court, the personal char-

acter of officials, the formation of American militia companies and their parades in the streets—all alike fed the flames of the Creoles' vehement indignation.

In March, 1804, Congress passed an act dividing the province into two parts on the present northern boundary of Louisiana, giving each a distinct government, and to the lower the title of the territory of Orleans. This act, which was to take effect the following October, interdicted the slave-trade. Then, indeed, anger burned. Insurrectionary sentiments were placarded on the street corners, crowds copied them, and public officers attempting to remove them were driven away. But that was all. Claiborne—young, like Bienville and like Galvez, but benevolent, wise, and patient—soon saw it was not the Government, but only some of its measures, that caused so much heat. The merchants, who in 1768 had incited revolt against legalized ruin, saw, now, on the other hand, that American rule had lifted them out of commercial serfdom, and that, as a port of the United States, and only as such, their crescent city could enter upon the great future which was hers by her geographical position. But we have seen that the merchants were not principally Creoles.

Although the Creoles looked for a French or Spanish re-cession, yet both interest and probability were so plainly against it that they were presently demanding impatiently, if not imperiously, the rights of American citizens as pledged to them in the treaty. They made no appeal to that France which had a second time cast them off; but at three public meetings, in June and July, petitioned Congress not to rescind the cession but to leave Louisiana undivided, and so hasten their admission into the Union. This appeal was fruitless, and the territorial government went into operation, Claiborne being retained as governor. The partition, the presidential appointment of a legislative council instead of its election by the people, the nullification of certain Spanish land grants, and an official re-inspection of all titles, were accepted, if not with patience, at least with that grace which the Creole assumes before the inevitable. But his respect was not always forthcoming toward laws that could be opposed or evaded. "This city," wrote Claiborne, "requires a strict police : the inhabitants are of various descriptions ; many highly respectable, and some of them very degenerate." A sheriff and posse attempted to arrest a Spanish officer. Two hundred men interfered; swords were drawn, and resistance ceased only when a detachment of United States troops were seen hurrying to the rescue. Above all, the slave-trade—" all-important to the existence of the country "—was diligently plied through the lakes and the inlets of Barataria.

The winter of 1804–05 was freer from bickerings than the last had been. The intrigues of Spanish officials who lingered in the district were unavailing, and the Governor reported a gratifying state of order. On the 2d of March, with many unwelcome safeguards and limitations,

the right was accorded the people to elect a House of
Representatives, and " to form for themselves a constitution and State government so soon as the free population

Rev. Father Antonio de Sedella (Père Antoine).

of the territory should reach sixty thousand souls, in order
to be admitted into the Union."

For a time following there was feverishness rather than
events. Great Britain and Spain were at war ; Havana
was open to neutral vessels ; the commerce of New Orleans was stimulated. But the pertinacious lingering of

10

Casa-Calvo, Morales, and others,—whom Claiborne at last had to force away in February, 1806,—the rumors they kept alive, the fear of war with Spain, doubts as to how the Creoles would or should stand, party strife among the Americans in New Orleans, and a fierce quarrel in the Church between the vicar-general and the famed Père Antoine, pastor of the cathedral, kept the public mind in a perpetual ferment. Still, in all these things there was only restiveness and discord, not revolution. The Creoles had at length undergone their last transplanting, and taken root in American privileges and principles. From the guilt of the plot whose events were now impending the Creole's hand is clean. We have Claiborne's testimony:

" Were it not for the calumnies of some Frenchmen who are among us, and the intrigues of a few ambitious, unprincipled men whose native language is English, I do believe that the Louisianians would be very soon the most zealous and faithful members of our republic."

On the 4th of November, 1811, a convention elected by the people of Orleans Territory met in New Orleans, and on the 28th of the following January adopted a State constitution ; and on the 30th of April, 1812, Louisiana entered the Union.

XXII.

ON one of those summer evenings when the Creoles, in the early years of the century, were wont to seek the river air in domestic and social groups under the willow and china trees of their levee, there glided around the last bend of the Mississippi above New Orleans " an elegant barge," equipped with sails and colors, and impelled by the stroke of ten picked oarsmen. It came down the harbor, drew in to the bank, and presently set ashore a small, slender, extremely handsome man, its only passenger. He bore letters from General Wilkinson, introducing him in New Orleans, and one, especially, to Daniel Clark, Wilkinson's agent, stating that " this great and honorable man would communicate to him many things improper to letter, and which he would not say to any other." Claiborne wrote to Secretary Madison, " Colonel Burr arrived in this city on this evening."

The date was June 26, 1805. The distinguished visitor, a day or two later, sat down to a banquet given to him by the unsuspecting Governor. He was now in full downward career. Only a few years before he had failed of the presidency by but one electoral vote. Only a few months had passed since, on completing his term, he had vacated the vice-presidency. In the last year of that term Alexander Hamilton had fallen by his hand. Friends and power, both, were lost. But he yet had strength in the West. Its people were still wild, restless, and eager for adventure. The conquest of " Orleans " was a traditional idea. Its banks were full of specie. Clouds of revolution were gathering all around the Gulf. The regions beyond the Red and the Sabine Rivers invited conquest. The earlier schemes of Adams and Hamilton, to seize Orleans Island and the Floridas for the United States ; that of Miranda, to expel the Spanish power from the farther shores of the Gulf ; the plottings of Wilkinson, to surrender the West into the hands of Spain—all these abandoned projects seem to have cast their shadows on the mind of Burr and colored his designs.

The stern patriotism of the older States had weighed him in its balances and rejected him. He had turned with a vagueness of plan that waited for clearer definition on the chances of the future, and, pledged to no principle, had set out in quest of aggrandizement and empire, either on the Mississippi or among the civilizations that encircle the Gulf of Mexico, as the turn of events might decree. In the West, he had met Wilkinson, and was now in correspondence with him.

The Governor who had feasted him moved much in the gay society of the Creoles. It was not giddiness, but anxious thought and care that pushed him into such scenes. Troubles and afflictions marked his footsteps; his wife and child stricken down by yellow fever, her young brother-in-law rashly championing him against the sneers of his enemies, fallen in a duel; but it was necessary to avoid the error—Ulloa's earlier error—of self-isolation. He wisely, therefore, mingled in the gayeties of the touchy people, even took from among them—after a short year of widowhood—a second wife, bore all things without resentment, and by thus studying the social side of the people, viewed public questions from behind.

The question ever before him—which he was incessantly asking himself, and which he showed an almost morbid wish to be always answering to the heads of departments at Washington—was whether the Creoles over whom he was set to rule were loyal to the government of the nation. It was a vital question. The bonds of the Union, even outside of Louisiana, were as yet slender and frail. The whole Mississippi valley was full of designing adventurers, suspected and unsuspected, ready to reap any advantage whatever of any disaffection of the people. He knew there were such in New Orleans.

The difficulty of answering this question lay in one single, broad difference between Claiborne himself and the civilization which he had been sent to reconstruct into harmony with North American thought and action. With him loyalty to the State meant obedience to its laws. The Creole had never been taught that there was any necessary connection between the two. The Governor's young Virginian spirit assumed it as self-evident that a man would either keep the laws or overturn them. It was a strange state of society to him, where one could be a patriot and yet ignore, evade, and override the laws of the country he loved. " Occasionally, in conversation with ladies,"—so he writes—" I have denounced smuggling as dishonest, and very generally a reply, in substance as follows, would be returned : ' That is impossible, for my grandfather, or my father, or my husband was, under the Spanish Government, a great smuggler, and he was always esteemed an honest man.'" They might have added, " and loyal to the king."

With some men Claiborne had had no trouble. " A beginning must be made," said Poydras, a wealthy and benevolent Frenchman ; " we must be initiated into the sacred duties of freemen and the practices of liberty." But the mass, both high and low, saw in the abandonment of smuggling or of the slave-trade only a surrender of existence—an existence to which their own consciences and the ladies at the ball gave them a clean patent. These, by their angry obduracy, harassed their governor with ungrounded fears of sedition.

In fact, the issue before governor and people was one to which the question of fealty to government was quite subordinate. It was the struggle of a North American against a Spanish American civilization. Burr must have seen this ; and probably at this date there was nothing clearly and absolutely fixed in his mind but this, that the former civilization had cast him off, and that he was about to offer himself to the latter. New events were to answer the Governor's haunting question, and to give a new phase to the struggle between these two civilizations in the Mississippi valley.

Colonel Burr remained in New Orleans ten or twelve days, receiving much social attention, and then left for St. Louis, saying he would return in October. But he did not appear.

During the winter the question of boundaries threatened war with Spain, and the anger of Spain rose high when, in February, 1806, Claiborne expelled her agents, the resplendent Casa-Calvo and the quarrelsome Morales, from the Territory. The Spanish governor of Florida retorted by stopping the transmission of the United States mails through that province. Outside, the Spaniards threatened; inside, certain Americans of influence did hardly less. The Creoles were again supine. Père Antoine, the beloved pastor of the cathedral, was suspected — unjustly — of sedition; Wilkinson with his forces was unaccountably idle. "All is not right," wrote Claiborne; "I know not whom to censure; but it seems to me that there is wrong somewhere."

The strange character of the Creole people perplexed and wearied Claiborne. Unstable and whimsical, public-spirited and sordid by turns, a display of their patriotism caused a certain day to be "among the happiest of his life;" and when autumn passed and toward its close their enthusiasm disappeared in their passion for money-getting, he " began to despair." But, alike unknown in the Creole town—to money-getters and to patriots—the only real danger had passed. Wilkinson had decided to betray Burr.

Late in September the General had arrived at Natchitoches, and had taken chief command of the troops confronting the Spanish forces. On the 8th of October, one Samuel Swartwout brought him a confidential letter from Colonel Burr. He was received by Wilkinson with much attention, stayed eight days, and then left for New Orleans. On the 21st, Wilkinson determined to expose the plot. He despatched a messenger to the President of the United States, bearing a letter which apprised him of Colonel Burr's contemplated descent of the Mississippi with an armed force. Eight days later, the General arranged with the Spaniards for the troops under each flag to withdraw from the contested boundary, leaving its location to be settled by the two governments, and hastened toward New Orleans, hurrying on in advance of him a force of artificers and a company of soldiers.

Presently the people of New Orleans were startled from apathetic tranquillity into a state of panic. All unexplained, these troops had arrived, others had re-enforced them ; there was hurried repair and preparation ; and the air was agitated with rumors. To Claiborne, the revelation had at length come from various directions that Aaron Burr was plotting treason. Thousands were said to be involved with him ; the first outbreak was expected to be in New Orleans.

Wilkinson had arrived in the town. In the bombastic style of one who plays a part, he demanded of Claiborne the proclamation of martial law. Claiborne kindly, and with expressions of confidence in the General, refused; but the two met the city's chamber of commerce, laid the plot before it, and explained the needs of defence. Several thousand dollars were at once subscribed, and a transient embargo of the port recommended, for the purpose of procuring sailors for the four gun-boats and two bomb-ketches lying in the harbor.

There were others in whose confidence Wilkinson held no place. The acting-governor of Mississippi wrote to Claiborne: " Should he [Colonel Burr] pass us, your fate will depend on the General, not on the Colonel. If I stop Burr, this may hold the General in his allegiance to the United States. But if Burr passes the territory with two thousand men, I have no doubt but the General will be your worst enemy. Be on your guard against the wily General. He is not much better than Catiline. Consider him a traitor and act as if certain thereof. You may save yourself by it."

On Sunday, the 14th of December, a Dr. Erick Bollman was arrested by Wilkinson's order. Swartwout and Ogden had already been apprehended at Fort Adams, and were then confined on one of the bomb-ketches in the harbor. On the 16th, a court officer, armed with writs of *habeas corpus*, sought in vain to hire a boat to carry him off to the bomb-ketch, and on the next day, when one could be procured, only Ogden could be found.

He was liberated, but only to be re-arrested with one Alexander, and held in the face of the *habeas corpus*. The court issued an attachment against Wilkinson. It was powerless. The Judge—Workman—appealed to Claiborne to sustain it with force. The Governor promptly declined, the Judge resigned, and Wilkinson ruled.

One of Burr's intimates was General Adair. On the 14th of January, 1807, he appeared in New Orleans unannounced. Colonel Burr, he said, with only a servant, would arrive in a few days. As he was sitting at dinner, his hotel was surrounded by regulars, an aide of Wilkinson appeared and arrested him ; he was confined, and presently was sent away. The troops beat to arms, regulars and militia paraded through the terrified city, and Judge Workman, with two others, were thrown into confinement. They were released within twenty-four hours ; but to intensify the general alarm, four hundred Spaniards from Pensacola arrived at the mouth of Bayou St. John, a few miles from the city, on their way to Baton Rouge, and their commander asked of Claiborne that he and his staff might pass through New Orleans. He was refused the liberty.

All this time the Creoles had been silent. Now, however, through their legislature, they addressed their governor. They washed their hands of the treason which threatened the peace and safety of Louisiana, but boldly announced their intention to investigate the " extraordinary measures " of Wilkinson and to complain to Congress.

Burr, meanwhile, with the mere nucleus of a force, had

set his expedition in motion, and at length, after twenty years' threatening by the Americans of the West, a fleet of boats actually bore an armed expedition down the Ohio and out into the Mississippi, bent on conquest.

But disaster lay in wait for it. It failed to gather strength as it came, and on the 28th of January the news reached New Orleans that Burr, having arrived at a point near Natchez with fourteen boats and about a hundred men, had been met by Mississippi militia, arrested, taken to Natchez, and released on bond to appear for trial at the next term of the Territorial Court.

This bond Burr ignored, and left the Territory. The Governor of Mississippi offered $2,000 for his apprehension, and on the 3d of March the welcome word came to New Orleans that he had been detected in disguise and re-arrested at Fort Stoddart, Alabama.

About the middle of May, Wilkinson sailed from New Orleans to Virginia to testify in that noted trial which, though it did not end in the conviction of Burr, made final wreck of his designs, restored public tranquillity, and assured the country of the loyalty not only of the West, but also of the Creoles of Louisiana. The struggle between the two civilizations withdrew finally into the narrowest limits of the Delta, and Spanish American thought found its next and last exponent in an individual without the ambition of empire,—a man polished, brave and chivalrous ; a patriot, and yet a contrabandist; an outlaw, and in the end a pirate.

XXIII.

BETWEEN 1804 and 1810, New Orleans doubled its population. The common notion is that there was a large influx of Anglo-Americans. This was not the case. A careful estimate shows not more than 3,100 of these in the city in 1809, yet in the following year the whole population, including the suburbs, was 24,552. The Americans, therefore, were numerically feeble. The increase came from another direction.

Napoleon's wars were convulsing Europe. The navies of his enemies fell upon the French West Indies. In Cuba large numbers of white and mulatto refugees who, in the St. Domingan insurrection, had escaped across to Cuba with their slaves, were now, by hostilities between France and Spain, forced again to become exiles. Within sixty days, between May and July, 1809, thirty-four vessels from Cuba set ashore in the streets of New Orleans nearly fifty-eight hundred persons—whites, free mulattoes, and black slaves in almost equal numbers. Others came later from Cuba, Guadaloupe, and other islands, until they amounted to ten thousand. Nearly all settled permanently in New Orleans.

The Creoles of Louisiana received the Creoles of the West Indies with tender welcomes. The state of society in the islands from which these had come needs no description. As late as 1871, '72, and '73, there were in the island of Guadaloupe only three marriages to a thousand inhabitants. But they came to their better cousins with the ties of a common religion, a common tongue, much common sentiment, misfortunes that may have had some resemblance, and with the poetry of exile. They were re-enforcements, too, at a moment when the power of the Americans—few in number, but potent in energies and advantages—was looked upon with hot jealousy.

The Anglo-Americans clamored against them, for they came in swarms. They brought little money or goods. They raised the price of bread and of rent. They lowered morals and disturbed order. Yet it was certainly true the Anglo-Americans had done little to improve either of these. Some had come to stay; many more to make a fortune and get away; both sorts were simply and only seeking wealth.

The West Indians had not come to a city whose civilization could afford to absorb them. The Creole element needed a better infusion, and yet it was probably the best in the community. The Spaniards were few and bad, described by one as capable of the vilest depredations, "a nuisance to the country," and even by the mild Claiborne

as " for the most part . . . well suited for mischiev-
ous and wicked enterprises." The free people of color
were about two thousand, unaspiring, corrupted, and
feeble. The floating population was extremely bad.
Sailors from all parts of the world took sides, according
to nationality, in bloody street riots and night brawls;
and bargemen, flat-boatmen, and raftsmen, from the wild
banks of the Ohio, Tennessee, and Cumberland, abandoned themselves at the end of their journey to the most
shameful and reckless excesses. The spirit of strife ran
up into the better classes. A newspaper article reflecting
upon Napoleon all but caused a riot. A public uprising
was hardly prevented when three young navy officers released a slave girl who was being whipped. In September, 1807, occurred the " batture riots." The *batture* was
the sandy deposits made by the Mississippi in front of the
Faubourg St. Marie. The noted jurist, Edward Livingston, representing private claimants, took possession of
this ground, and was opposed by the public in two distinct outbreaks. In the second, the Creoles, ignoring the
decision of the Supreme Court, rallied to the spot by
thousands, and were quieted only by the patient appeals
of Claiborne, addressed to them on the spot, and by the
recommittal of the contest to the United States courts, in
whose annals it is so well-known a cause. Preparations
for war with Spain heightened the general fever. Claiborne's letters dwell on the sad mixture of society.
" England," he writes, " has her partisans; Ferdinand

the Seventh, some faithful subjects; Bonaparte, his admirers; and there is a fourth description of men, commonly called *Burrites*, who would join any standard which would promise rapine and plunder." These last had a newspaper, "La Lanterne Magique," whose libels gave the executive much anxiety.

In Rue du Maine.

Now, into such a city—say of fourteen thousand inhabitants, at most—swarm ten thousand white, yellow, and black West India islanders; some with means, others in absolute destitution, and "many . . . of doubtful character and desperate fortune." Americans, English,

Spanish, cry aloud; the laws forbid the importation of slaves; Claiborne adjures the American consuls at Havana and Santiago de Cuba to stop the movement; the free people of color are ordered point-blank to leave the country; the actual effort is made to put the order into execution; and still all three classes continue to pour into the streets, to throw themselves upon the town's hospitality, and daily to increase the cost of living and the number of distressed poor.

They came and they stayed, in Orleans Street, in Du Maine, St. Philippe, St. Peter, Dauphine, Burgundy, and the rest, all too readily dissolving into the corresponding parts of the native Creole community, and it is easier to underestimate than to exaggerate the silent results of an event that gave the French-speaking Louisianians twice the numerical power with which they had begun to wage their long battle against American absorption.

XXIV.

IT has already been said that the whole Gulf coast of
Louisiana is sea-marsh. It is an immense, wet, level
expanse, covered everywhere, shoulder-high, with marsh-
grasses, and indented by extensive bays that receive the
rivers and larger bayous. For some sixty miles on either
side of the Mississippi's mouth, it breaks into a grotesque-
ly contorted shore-line and into bright archipelagoes of
hundreds of small, reedy islands, with narrow and obscure channels writhing hither and thither between them.
These mysterious passages, hidden from the eye that
overglances the seemingly unbroken sunny leagues of surrounding distance, are threaded only by the far-seen
white or red lateen-sail of the oyster-gatherer, or by the
pirogue of the hunter stealing upon the myriads of wild
fowl that in winter haunt these vast green wastes.

To such are known the courses that enable them to
avoid the frequent *culs-de-sac* of the devious shore, and
that lead to the bayous which open the way to the inhabited interior. They lead through miles of clear, brown,
silent waters, between low banks fringed with dwarf oaks,
11

across pale green distances of "quaking prairie," in whose
shallow, winding *coolées* the smooth, dark, shining needles
of the round rush stand twelve feet high to overpeer the
bulrushes, and at length, under the solemn shades of cypress swamps, to the near neighborhood of the Mississippi,
from whose flood the process of delta-growth has cut the
bayou off.   Across the mouths of the frequent bays that
indent this marshy coast-line stretch long, slender keys of
dazzling, storm-heaped sand—sometimes of cultivable soil.

About sixty miles south from the bank of the Mississippi as that river flows eastward by New Orleans, lies
Grande Terre, a very small island of this class, scarce two
miles long, and a fourth as wide, stretching across two-thirds
of the entrance of Barataria Bay, but leaving a pass of about
a mile width at its western end, with a navigable channel.
Behind this island the waters of the bay give a safe, deep
harbor.   At the west of the bay lies a multitude of small,
fenny islands, interwoven with lakes, bays, and passes,
named and unnamed, affording cunning exit to the bayous
La Fourche and Terre Bonne and the waters still beyond.
They are populous beyond estimate with the prey of
fowler and fisherman, and of the huge cormorant, the gull,
the man-of-war bird, the brown pelican and the alba-
tross.   Here in his time the illustrious Creole nat-
uralist, Audubon, sought and found in great multitude the white pelican, now so rare, that rose at the
sound of his gun and sailed unwillingly away on wings
that measured eight feet and a half from tip to tip.

Northward the bay extends some sixteen miles, and then breaks in every direction across the illimitable wet prairies into lakes and bayous. Through one of these—the bayou Barataria, with various other local names—a way opens irregularly northward. Now and then it widens into a lake, and narrows again, each time more than the last, the leagues of giant reeds and rushes are left behind, a few sugar and rice plantations are passed, standing, lonely and silent, in the water and out of the water, the dark shadows of the moss-hung swamp close down, and the stream's windings become more and more difficult, until near its head a short canal is entered on the right, and six miles farther on the forest opens, you pass between two plantations, and presently are stopped abruptly by the levee of the Mississippi. You mount its crown, and see, opposite, the low-lying city, with its spires peering up from the sunken plain, its few wreaths of manufactory smoke, and the silent stir of its winding harbor. Canal Street, its former upper boundary, is hidden two miles and a half away down the stream. There are other Baratarian routes, through lakes Salvador or Des Allemands, and many obscure avenues of return toward the Gulf of Mexico or the maze of wet lands intervening.

In the first decade of the century the wars of France had filled this gulf with her privateers. Spain's rich commerce was the prey around which they hovered, and Guadaloupe and Martinique their island haunts. From these the English, operating in the West Indies, drove them out, and when in February, 1810, Guadaloupe completed the list of their conquests, the French privateers were as homeless as Noah's raven.

They were exiled on the open Gulf, with the Spaniards lining its every shore, except one, where American neutrality motioned them austerely away. This was Louisiana. But this, of all shores, suited them best. Thousands of their brethren already filled the streets of New Orleans, and commanded the sympathies of the native Creoles. The tangled water-ways of Barataria, so well known to smugglers and slavers, and to so few beside, leading by countless windings and intersections to the markets of the thriving city, offered the rarest facilities for their purposes. Between this shelter and the distant harbors of France there could be no question of choice.

Hither they came, fortified Grande Terre, built storehouses, sailed away upon the Gulf, and re-appeared with prizes which it seems were not always Spanish. The most seductive auctions followed. All along this coast there are vast heaps of a species of clam-shell, too great to admit the idea of their being other than the work of nature. Great oaks grow on them. The aborigines, mound-builders, used these places for temple-sites. One of them, in Barataria, distinguished from larger neighbors by the name of Petit Temple, "the Little Temple," removed of late years for the value of its shells as a paving material, yielded three hundred thousand barrels of them. A notable group of these mounds, on one of the larger

islands of Barataria, became the privateers' chief place of
sale and barter. It was known as the Temple. There
was no scarcity of buyers from New Orleans and the surrounding country. Goods were also smuggled up the
various bayous, especially La Fourche. Then the captured vessels were burned or refitted, sails were spread
again, and prows were pointed toward the Spanish Main.
The Baratarians had virtually revived, in miniature, the
life of the long-extinct buccaneers.

On the beautiful, wooded, grassy and fertile "Grande
Isle," lying just west of their stronghold on "Grande
Terre," and separated from it only by the narrow pass
that led out to sea, storehouses and dwellings were built,
farms and orangeries yielded harvests, and green meadows
dotted with wax-myrtles, casinos, and storm-dwarfed oaks
rose from the marshy inland side where the children and
women plied their shrimp and crab nets, and, running
down to the surf-beach on the southern side, looked
across the boundless open Gulf toward the Spanish Main.

The fame of the Baratarians spread far and wide ; and
while in neighboring States the scandalous openness of
their traffic brought loud condemnation upon Louisiana
citizens and officials alike, the merchants and planters of
the Delta, profiting by these practices, with the general
public as well, screened the contrabandists and defended
their character.

Much ink has been spilled from that day to this to
maintain that they sailed under letters of marque. But

certainly no commission could be worth the unrolling when carried by men who had removed themselves beyond all the restraints that even seem to distinguish privateering from piracy. They were often overstocked with vessels and booty, but they seem never to have been embarrassed with the care of prisoners.

There lived at this time, in New Orleans, John and Pierre Lafitte. John, the younger, but more conspicuous of the two, was a handsome man, fair, with black hair and eyes, wearing his beard, as the fashion was, shaven neatly away from the front of his face. His manner was generally courteous, though he was irascible and in graver moments somewhat harsh. He spoke fluently English, Spanish, Italian, and French, using them with much affability at the hotel where he resided, and indicating, in the peculiarities of his French, his nativity in the city of Bordeaux.

The elder brother was a seafaring man and had served in the French navy. He appears to have been every way less showy than the other; but beyond doubt both men were above the occupation with which they began life in Louisiana. This was the trade of blacksmith, though at their forge, on the corner of St. Philip and Bourbon Streets, probably none but slave hands swung the sledge or shaped the horseshoe.

It was during the embargo, enforced by the United States Government in 1808, that John Lafitte began to be a merchant. His store was in Royal Street, where, behind a show of legitimate trade, he was busy running the embargo with goods and Africans. He wore the disguise carelessly. He was cool and intrepid and had only the courts to evade, and his unlawful adventures did not lift his name from the published lists of managers of society balls or break his acquaintance with prominent legislators.

In 1810 came the West Indian refugees and the Guadaloupian privateers. The struggle between the North American and the West Indian ideas of public order and morals took new energy on the moment. The plans of the "set of bandits who infested the coast and overran the country" were described by Government as "extensive and well laid," and the confession made that "so general seemed the disposition to aid in their concealment, that but faint hopes were entertained of detecting the parties and bringing them to justice."

Their trade was impudently open. Merchants gave and took orders for their goods in the streets of the town as frankly as for the merchandise of Philadelphia or New York. Frequent seizures lent zest to adventure without greatly impairing the extravagant profits of a commerce that paid neither duties nor first cost.

John and Pierre Lafitte became the commercial agents of the "privateers." By and by they were their actual chiefs. They won great prosperity for the band; prizes were rich and frequent, and slave cargoes profitable. John Lafitte did not at this time go to sea. He equipped vessels, sent them on their cruises, sold their prizes and slaves, and moved hither and thither throughout the Delta, administering affairs with boldness and sagacity. The Mississippi's "coasts" in the parishes of St. James and St. John the Baptist were often astir with his known presence, and his smaller vessels sometimes pierced the interior as far as Lac des Allemands. He knew the value of popular admiration, and was often at country balls, where he enjoyed the fame of great riches and courage, and seduced many of the simple Acadian youth to sail in his cruises. His two principal captains were Beluche and Dominique You. " Captain Dominique" was small, graceful, fair, of a pleasant, even attractive face, and a skilful sailor. There were also Gambi, a handsome Italian, who died only a few years ago at the old pirate village of Chenière Caminada ; and Rigoult, a dark Frenchman, whose ancient house still stands on Grande Isle. And yet again Johnness and Johannot, unless—which appears likely—these were only the real names of Dominique and Beluche.

Expeditions went out against these men more than once ; but the Government was pre-occupied and embarrassed, and the expeditions seemed feebly conceived. They only harassed the Baratarians, drove them to the mouth of La Fourche in vessels too well armed to be attacked in transports, and did not prevent their prompt return to Grande Terre.

The revolution for the independence of the Colombian States of South America began. Venezuela declared her independence in July, 1811. The Baratarians procured letters of marque from the patriots in Carthagena, lowered the French flag, ran up the new standard, and thus far and no farther joined the precarious fortunes of the new states, while Barataria continued to be their haunt and booty their only object.

They reached the height of their fortune in 1813. Their moral condition had declined in proportion. "Among them," says the Governor, "are some St. Domingo negroes of the most desperate character, and no worse than most of their white associates." Their avowed purpose, he says, was to cruise on the high seas and commit "depredations and piracies on the vessels of nations in peace with the United States."

One of these nations was the British. Its merchantmen were captured in the Gulf and sold behind Grande Terre. The English more than once sought redress with their own powder and shot. On the 23d of June, 1813, a British sloop-of-war anchored off the outer end of the channel at the mouth of La Fourche and sent her boats to attack two privateers lying under the lee of Cat Island; but the pirates stood ground and repulsed them with considerable loss.

Spain, England, and the United States were now their enemies; yet they grew bolder and more outrageous. Smuggling increased. The Government was "set at defiance in broad daylight." "I remember," reads a manuscript kindly furnished the present writer, "when three

Spanish vessels were brought in to Caillou Islands. They were laden with a certain Spanish wine, and the citizens of Attakapas went out to see them and purchased part of the captured cargoes. There were no traces of the former crews."

In October, 1813, a revenue officer seized some contraband goods near New Orleans. He was fired upon by a party under John Lafitte, one of his men wounded, and the goods taken from him. The Governor offered $500 for Lafitte's apprehension, but without avail.

In January, 1814, four hundred and fifteen negroes, consigned to John and Pierre Lafitte, were to be auctioned at " The Temple." An inspector of customs and twelve men were stationed at the spot. John Lafitte attacked them, killed the inspector, wounded two men, and made the rest prisoners.

Still he was not arrested. His island was fortified, his schooners and feluccas were swift, his men were well organized and numbered four hundred, the Federal Government was getting the worst of it in war with Great Britain, and, above all, the prevalence of West Indian ideas in New Orleans was a secure shelter. He sent his spoils daily up La Fourche to Donaldsonville on the Mississippi, and to other points. Strong, well-armed escorts protected them. Claiborne asked the legislature to raise one hundred men for six months' service. The request was neglected. At the same time a filibustering expedition against Texas was only stopped by energetic measures. The Federal courts could effect nothing. An expedition captured both Lafittes, but they disappeared, and the writs were returned "not found."

But now the tide turned. Society began to repudiate the outlaws. In July, 1814, a grand jury denounced them as pirates, and exhorted the people " to remove the stain that has fallen on all classes of society in the minds of the good people of the sister States." Indictments were found against Johnness and Johannot for piracies in the Gulf, and against Pierre Lafitte as accessory. Lafitte was arrested, bail was refused, and he found himself at last shut up in the calaboza.

XXV.

BARATARIA DESTROYED.

WEIGHING all the facts, it is small wonder that the Delta Creoles coquetted with the Baratarians. To say no more of Spanish American or French West Indian tincture, there was the Embargo. There were the warships of Europe skimming ever to and fro in the entrances and exits of the Gulf. Rarely in days of French or Spanish rule had this purely agricultural country and non-manufacturing town been so removed to the world's end as just at this time. The Mississippi, northward, was free; but its perils had hardly lessened since the days of Spanish rule. Then it was said, in a curious old Western advertisement of 1797, whose English is worthy of notice:

"No danger need be apprehended from the enemy, as every person whatever will be under cover, made proof against rifle or musket balls, and convenient port-holes for firing out of. Each of the boats are armed with six pieces, carry a pound ball, also a number of muskets, and amply supplied with plenty of ammunition, strongly manned with choice hands, and masters of approved knowledge."

Scarcely any journey, now, outside of Asia, Africa, and the Polar seas, is more arduous than was then the trip from St. Louis to New Orleans. Vagabond Indians, white marauders, Spanish-armed extortion and arrest, and the natural perils of the stream, made the river little, if any, less dangerous than the Gulf. Culbert and Maglibray were the baser Lafittes of the Mississippi, and Cotton-wood Creek their Barataria.

And the labors and privations were greater than the dangers. The conveyances were keel-boats, barges, and flat-boats. The flat-boats, at New Orleans, were broken up for their lumber, their slimy gunwales forming along the open gutter's edge in many of the streets a narrow and treacherous substitute for a pavement. The keel-boats and barges returned up-stream, propelled now by sweeps and now by warping or by *cordelle* (hand tow-ropes), consuming "three or four months of the most painful toil that can be imagined." Exposure and bad diet "ordinarily destroyed one-third of the crew."

But on the 10th of January, 1812, there had pushed in to the landing at New Orleans a sky-blue thing with a long bowsprit, "built after the fashion of a ship, with port-holes in the side," and her cabin in the hold. She was the precursor of the city's future greatness, the *Orleans*, from Pittsburg, the first steam vessel on the Mississippi.

Here was a second freedom of the great river mightier than that wrested from Spain. Commercial grandeur seemed just at hand. All Spanish America was asserting its independence; Whitney's genius was making cotton the world's greatest staple; immigrants were swarming into the West; the Mississippi valley would be the provision-house of Europe, the importer of untold millions of manufactures; New Orleans would keep the only gate. Instead of this, in June, 1812, Congress declared war against Great Britain. Barataria seemed indispensable, and New Orleans was infested with dangers.

In 1813, Wilkinson, still commanding in the West, marched to Mobile River; in April he drove the Spaniards out of Fort Charlotte and raised a small fortification, Fort Bowyer, to command the entrance of Mobile Bay. Thus the Spanish, neighbors only less objectionable than the British, were crowded back to Pensacola. But, this done, Wilkinson was ordered to the Canadian frontier, and even took part of his few regulars with him.

The English were already in the Gulf; the Indians were growing offensive; in July seven hundred crossed the Perdido into Mississippi; in September they massacred three hundred and fifty whites at Fort Mimms, and opened the Creek war. Within New Orleans bands of drunken Choctaws roamed the streets. The Baratarians were seen daily in the public resorts. Incendiary fires became alarmingly common, and the *batture* troubles again sprang up. Naturally, at such a junction, Lafitte and his men reached the summit of power.

In February, 1814, four hundred country militia reported at Magazine Barracks, opposite New Orleans. The

Governor tried to force out the city militia. He got only clamorous denunciation and refusal to obey. The country muster offered their aid to enforce the order. The city companies heard of it, and only Claiborne's discreetness averted the mortifying disaster of a battle without an enemy. The country militia, already deserting, was disbanded. Even the legislature withheld its support, and Claiborne was everywhere denounced as a traitor. He had to report to the President his complete failure. Still, he insisted apologetically, the people were emphatically ready to "turn out in case of actual invasion." Only so patient a man could understand that the Creoles were conscientious in their lethargy. Fortunately the invasion did not come until the Creek war had brought to view the genius of Andrew Jackson.

In April, Government raised the embargo. But the relief was tardy ; the banks suspended. Word came that Paris had fallen. Napoleon had abdicated. England would throw new vigor into the war with America, and could spare troops for the conquest of Louisiana.

In August the Creeks made peace. Some British officers landed at Apalachicola, Florida, bringing artillery. Some disaffected Creeks joined them and were by them armed and drilled. But now, at length, the Government took steps to defend the Southwest.

General Jackson was given the undertaking. He wrote to Claiborne to hold his militia ready to march—an order very easy to give. In September he repaired to Mobile, which was already threatened. The British Colonel Nicholls had landed at Pensacola with some companies of infantry, from two sloops-of-war. The officers from Apalachicola and a considerable body of Indians had joined him, without objection from the Spaniards.

Suddenly attention was drawn to the Baratarians. On the third of September an armed brig had appeared off Grande Terre. She fired on an inbound vessel, forcing her to run aground, tacked, and presently anchored some six miles from shore. Certain of the islanders went off in a boat, ventured too near, and, turning to retreat, were overhauled by the brig's pinnace, carrying British colors and a white flag. In the pinnace were two naval officers and a captain of infantry. They asked for Mr. Lafitte, one officer speaking in French for the other.

"He is ashore," said the chief person in the island boat, a man of dignified and pleasing address. The officers handed him a packet addressed "To Mr. Lafitte, Barataria," and asked that it be carefully delivered to him in person. The receiver of it, however, induced them to continue on, and when they were plainly in his power revealed himself.

"I, myself, am Mr. Lafitte." As they drew near the shore, he counselled them to conceal their business from his men. More than two hundred Baratarians lined the beach clamoring for the arrest of the "spies," but Lafitte contrived to get them safely to his dwelling, quieted his men, and opened the packet.

There were four papers in it. First, Colonel Nicholls's appeal to the Creoles to help restore Louisiana to Spain; to Spaniards, French, Italians, and Britons, to aid in abolishing American usurpation; and to Kentuckians, to exchange supplies for money, and neutrality for an open Mississippi. Second, his letter to Lafitte offering a naval captain's commission to him, lands to all his followers, and protection in persons and property to all, if the pirates, with their fleet, would put themselves under the British naval commander, and announcing the early invasion of Louisiana with a powerful force. Third, an order from the naval commander in Pensacola Bay, to Captain Lockyer, the bearer of the packet, to procure restitution at Barataria for certain late piracies, or to "carry destruction over the whole place;" but also repeating Colonel Nicholls's overtures. And fourth, a copy of the orders under which Captain Lockyer had come. He was to secure the Baratarians' co-operation in an attack on Mobile, or, at all events, their neutrality. According to Lafitte, the captain added verbally the offer of $30,000 and many other showy inducements.

Lafitte asked time to consider. He withdrew; when in a moment the three officers and their crew were seized by the pirates and imprisoned. They were kept in confinement all night. In the morning Lafitte appeared, and, with many apologies for the rudeness of his men, conducted the officers to their pinnace, and they went off to the brig. The same day he addressed a letter to Captain

12

Lockyer asking a fortnight to " put his affairs in order," when he would be " entirely at his disposal." It is noticeable for its polished dignity and the purity of its English.

Was this anything more than stratagem ? The Spaniard and Englishman were his foe and his prey. The Creoles were his friends. His own large interests were scattered all over Lower Louisiana. His patriotism has been overpraised ; and yet we may allow him patriotism. His whole war, on the main-land side, was only with a set of ideas not superficially fairer than his own. They seemed to him unsuited to the exigencies of the times and the country. Thousands of Louisianians thought as he did. They and he—to borrow from a distance the phrase of another—were "polished, agreeable, dignified, averse to baseness and vulgarity." They accepted friendship, honor, and party faith as sufficient springs of action, and only dispensed with the sterner question of right and wrong. True, Pierre, his brother, and Dominique, his most intrepid captain, lay then in the calaboza. Yet should he, so able to take care of himself against all comers and all fates, so scornful of all subordination, for a paltry captain's commission and a doubtful thirty thousand, help his life-time enemies to invade the country and city of his commercial and social intimates ?

He sat down and penned a letter to his friend Blanque, of the legislature, and sent the entire British packet, asking but one favor, the "amelioration of the situation of his unhappy brother;" and the next morning one of the New Orleans papers contained the following advertisement:

$1,000 REWARD

WILL be paid for the apprehending of PIERRE LAFITTE, who broke and escaped last night from the prison of the parish. Said Pierre Lafitte is about five feet ten inches height, stout made, light complexion, and somewhat cross-eyed, further description is considered unnecessary, as he is very well known in the city.

Said Lafitte took with him three negroes, to wit: [giving their names and those of their owners]; the above reward will be paid to any person delivering the said Lafitte to the subscriber.

J. H. HOLLAND,

Keeper of the Prison.

On the 7th, John Lafitte wrote again to Blanque,—the British brig and two sloops-of-war still hovered in the offing,—should he make overtures to the United States Government? Blanque's advice is not known; but on the 10th, Lafitte made such overtures by letter to Claiborne, inclosed in one from Pierre Lafitte—who had joined him—to M. Blanque.

The outlawed brothers offered themselves and their men to defend Barataria, asking only oblivion of the past. The high-spirited periods of John Lafitte challenge admiration, even while they betray tinges of sophistry that may or may not have been apparent to their writer. "All the offence I have committed," wrote he, "I was forced to by certain vices in our laws." He did not say that these vices consisted mainly of enactments against smuggling, piracy, and the slave-trade.

The heads of the small naval and military force then near New Orleans were Commodore Paterson and Colonel Ross. They had organized and were hurriedly preparing a descent upon the Baratarians. A general of the Creole militia was Villeré, son of the unhappy patriot of 1768. Claiborne, with these three officers, met in council, with the Lafittes' letters and the British overtures before them, and debated the question whether the pirates' services should be accepted. Claiborne being in the chair was not called upon for a vote. It would be interesting to know, what, with his now thorough knowledge of the Creole character and all the expediencies of the situation, his vote would have been. Villeré voted yea, but Ross and Paterson stoutly nay, and thus it was decided. Nor did the British send ashore for Lafitte's final answer. They only lingered distantly for some days and then vanished.

Presently the expedition of Ross and Paterson was ready. Stealing down the Mississippi, it was joined at the mouth by some gun-vessels, sailed westward into the Gulf, and headed for Barataria. There was the schooner *Carolina*, six gun-vessels, a tender, and a launch. On the 16th of September they sighted Grande Terre, formed in line of battle, and stood for the entrance of the bay.

Within the harbor, behind the low island, the pirate fleet was soon descried forming in line. Counting all, schooners and feluccas, there were ten vessels. Two miles

Baratarian Luggers at the Fruit Landing.

from shore the *Carolina* was stopped by shoal water, and the two heavier gun-vessels grounded. But armed boats were launched, and the attack entered the pass and moved on into the harbor.

Soon two of the Baratarians' vessels were seen to be on fire; another, attempting to escape, grounded, and the pirates, except a few brave leaders, were flying. One of the fired vessels burned, the other was boarded and saved, the one which grounded got off again and escaped. All the rest were presently captured. At this moment, a fine, fully armed schooner appeared outside the island, was chased and taken. Scarcely was this done when another showed herself to eastward. The *Carolina* gave chase. The stranger stood for Grande Terre, and ran into water where the *Carolina* could not follow. Four boats were launched; whereupon the chase opened fire on the *Carolina*, and the gun-vessels in turn upon the chase, firing across the island from inside, and in half an hour she surrendered. She proved to be the *General Bolivar*, armed with one eighteen, two twelve, and one six-pounder.

The nest was broken up. "All their buildings and establishments at Grande Terre and Grand Isle, with their telegraph and stores at Chenière Caminada, were destroyed. On the last day of September, the elated squadron, with their prizes—seven cruisers of Lafitte, and three armed schooners under Carthagenian colors—arrived in New Orleans harbor amid the peal of guns from the old barracks and Fort St. Charles.

But among the prisoners the commanding countenance of John Lafitte and the cross-eyed visage of his brother Pierre were not to be seen. Both men had escaped up Bayou La Fourche to the "German Coast." Others who had had like fortune by and by gathered on Last Island, some sixty miles west of Grande Terre, and others found asylum in New Orleans, where they increased the fear of internal disorder.

XXVI.

THE BRITISH INVASION.

PATERSON and Ross had struck the Baratarians just in time. The fortnight asked of the British by Lafitte expired the next day. The British themselves were far away eastward, drawing off from an engagement of the day before, badly worsted. A force of seven hundred British troops, six hundred Indians, and four vessels of war had attacked Fort Bowyer, commanding the entrances of Mobile Bay and Mississippi Sound. Its small garrison had repulsed them and they retired again to Pensacola with serious loss, including a sloop-of-war grounded and burned.

Now General Jackson gathered four thousand men on the Alabama River, regulars, Tennesseeans, and Mississippi dragoons, and early in November attacked Pensacola with great spirit, took the two forts—which the Spaniards had allowed the English to garrison—drove the English to their shipping and the Indians into the interior, and returned to Mobile. Here he again called on Claiborne to muster his militia. Claiborne convened the Legislature and laid the call before it.

His was not the master-spirit to command a people so
different from himself in a moment of extremity. On
every side was discord, apprehension, and despondency
that he could not cure. Two committees of safety engaged in miserable disputes. Credit was destroyed.
Money commanded three or four per cent. a month.
The Legislature dawdled until the Louisianian himself
uttered a noble protest. "No other evidence of patriotism is to be found," cried Louallier, of Opelousas, "than a
disposition to avoid every expense, every fatigue."

It was easy to count up the resources of defence : Paterson's feeble navy, the weak Fort St. Philip on the
river, the unfinished Fort Petites Coquilles on the Rigo-
lets, Ross's seven hundred regulars, a thousand militia
mustered at last after three imperative calls, a wretchedly
short supply of ammunition—nothing more. "Our situation," says La Carriere Latour in his admirable memoir,
"seemed desperate." Twelve thousand chosen British
troops were known to have sailed for Louisiana.

But suddenly, one day, the first of winter, confidence
returned ; enthusiasm sprang up ; all was changed in a
moment by the arrival of one man, whose spare form
thrilled everything with its electric energy. He reviewed
the Creole troops, and praised their equipment and drill ;
he inspected their forts ; he was ill, but he was everywhere ; and everyone who saw that intense eye, that un-
furrowed but fixed brow, the dry locks falling down over
it as if blown there by hard riding, and the two double

side lines which his overwhelming and perpetual "must and shall" had dug at either corner of his firm but passionate mouth, recognized the master of the hour, and emulated his confidence and activity. Like the Creoles themselves, brave, impetuous, patriotic, and a law unto himself, and yet supplying the qualities they lacked, the continent could hardly have furnished a man better fitted to be their chief in a day of peril than was Andrew Jackson.

Soon the whole militia of city and State were added to the first thousand, organized and ready to march. There was another spring to their tardy alacrity. Eighty British ships, it was said, were bearing down toward Ship Island. Cochrane, the scourge of the Atlantic coast, was admiral of the fleet. On the 14th of December forty-five barges, carrying forty-three guns and one thousand two hundred British troops, engaged the weak American flotilla of six small vessels near the narrow passes of Lake Borgne. There was a short, gallant struggle, and the British were masters of the lake and its shores.

Even then the Legislature pronounced against Claiborne's recommendation that it declare martial law and adjourn. But Jackson instantly proclaimed it in ringing words. "The district's safety," he said, "must and will be maintained with the best blood of the country," and he would "separate the country's friends from its enemies."

Measures of defence were pushed on. Forts and stockades were manned, new companies and battalions were mustered, among them one of Choctaw Indians and two of free men of color. The jails were emptied to swell the ranks.

And hereupon John Lafitte, encouraged by Claiborne and the Legislature, came forward again. Jackson in one of his proclamations had called the Baratarians "hellish banditti," whose aid he spurned. But now these two intrepid leaders met face to face in a room that may still be pointed out in the old cabildo, and the services of Lafitte and his skilled artillerists were offered and accepted for the defence of the city. All proceedings against them were suspended; some were sent to man the siege-guns of Forts Petites Coquilles, St. John, and St. Philip, and others were enrolled in a body of artillery under "Captains" Beluche and Dominique. One of the General's later reports alludes to the Baratarians as "these gentlemen."

XXVII.

THE BATTLE OF NEW ORLEANS.

ONCE more the Creoles sang the "Marseillaise." The invaders hovering along the marshy shores of Lake Borgne were fourteen thousand strong. Sir Edward Packenham, brother-in-law to the Duke of Wellington, and a gallant captain, was destined to lead them. Gibbs, Lambert, and Kean were his generals of division. As to Jackson, thirty-seven hundred Tennesseeans under Generals Coffee and Carroll, had, when it was near Christmas, given him a total of but six thousand men. Yet confidence, animation, concord, and even gaiety, filled the hearts of the mercurial people.

"The citizens," says the eye-witness, Latour, "were preparing for battle as cheerfully as for a party of pleasure. The streets resounded with 'Yankee Doodle,' 'La Marseillaise,' 'Le Chant du Départ,' and other martial airs. The fair sex presented themselves at the windows and balconies to applaud the troops going through their evolutions, and to encourage their husbands, sons, fathers, and brothers to protect them from their enemies."

That enemy, reconnoitring on Lake Borgne, soon found in the marshes of its extreme western end the mouth of a navigable stream, the Bayou Bienvenue. This water flowed into the lake directly from the west— the direction of New Orleans, close behind whose lower suburb it had its beginning in a dense cypress swamp. Within its mouth it was over a hundred yards wide, and more than six feet deep. As they ascended its waters, everywhere, as far as the eye could reach, stretched only the unbroken quaking prairie. But soon they found and bribed a village of Spanish and Italian fishermen, and under their guidance explored the whole region. By turning into a smaller bayou, a branch of the first, the Mississippi was found a very few miles away on the left, hidden from view by a narrow belt of swamp and hurrying southeastward toward the Gulf. From the plantations of sugar-cane on its border, various draining canals ran back northward to the bayou, offering on their margins a fair though narrow walking way through the wooded and vine-tangled morass to the open plains on the river shore, just below New Orleans. By some oversight, which has never been explained, this easy route to the city's very outskirts had been left unobstructed. On the 21st of December some Creole scouts posted a picket at the fishermen's village.

The traveller on the New Orleans & Mobile Railroad, as he enters the southeastern extreme of Louisiana, gliding along the low, wet prairie margin of the Gulf, passes across an island made by the two mouths of Pearl River. It rises just high enough above the surrounding marsh to be at times tolerably dry ground. A sportsmen's station on it is called English Look-out; but the island itself seems to have quite lost its name. It was known then as Isle aux Poix (Pea Island). Here on December the 21st, 1814, the British had been for days disembarking. Early on the 22d General Kean's division re-embarked from this island in barges, shortly before dawn of the 23d captured the picket at the fishers' village, pushed on up the bayou, turned to the left, southwestward, into the smaller bayou (Mazant), entered the swamp, disembarked once more at the mouth of a plantation canal, marched southward along its edge through the wood, and a little before noon emerged upon the open plain of the river shore, scarcely seven miles from New Orleans, without a foot of fortification between them and the city. But the captured pickets had reported Jackson's forces eighteen thousand strong, and the British halted, greatly fatigued, until they should be joined by other divisions.

Not, however, to rest. At about two o'clock in the afternoon, while the people of the city were sitting at their midday dinner, suddenly the cathedral bell startled them with its notes of alarm, drums sounded the long-roll, and as military equipments were hurriedly put on, and Creoles, Americans, and San Domingans, swords and muskets in hand, poured in upon the Place d'Armes from every direction and sought their places in the ranks, word

passed from mouth to mouth that there had been a blun-
der, and that the enemy was but seven miles away in
force—"*sur l'habitation Villeré !*"—"on Villeré's plantation!" But courage was in every heart. Quickly the
lines were formed, the standards were unfurled, the huzza
resounded as the well-known white horse of Jackson came
galloping down their front with his staff—Edward Livingston and Abner Duncan among them—at his heels, the
drums sounded quickstep and the columns moved down
through the streets and out of the anxious town to meet
the foe. In half an hour after the note of alarm the
Seventh regulars, with two pieces of artillery and some
marines, had taken an advanced position. An hour and
a half later General Coffee, with his Tennessee and Mississippi cavalry, took their place along the small Rodriguez
canal, that ran from the river's levee to and into the
swamp, and which afterward became Jackson's permanent
line of defence. Just as the sun was setting the troops
that had been stationed at Bayou St. John, a battalion of
free colored men, then the Forty-fourth regulars, and then
the brightly uniformed Creole battalion, first came into
town by way of the old Bayou Road, and swept through the
streets toward the enemy on the run, glittering with accou-
trements and arms, under the thronged balconies and amid
the tears and plaudits of Creole mothers and daughters.

Night came on, very dark. The *Carolina* dropped noise-
lessly down opposite the British camp, anchored close in
shore, and opened her broadsides and musketry at short

range. A moment later Jackson fell upon the startled
foe with twelve hundred men and two pieces of artillery,
striking them first near the river shore, and presently
along their whole line.   Coffee, with six hundred men,
unseen in the darkness, issued from the woods on the
north, and attacked the British right, just as it was trying
to turn Jackson's left—Creole troops, whose ardor would
have led them to charge with the bayonet, but for the
prudence of the Regular officer in command.   A fog rose,
the smoke of battle rested on the field, the darkness thick-
ened, and all was soon in confusion.   Companies and battalions — red coats, blue coats, Highland plaidies, and
"dirty shirts" (Tennesseeans), from time to time got lost,
fired into friendly lines, or met their foes in hand to hand
encounters.   Out in the distant prairie behind the swamp
forest the second division of the British coming on, heard
the battle, hurried forward, and began to reach the spot
while the low plain, wrapped in darkness, was still flashing
with the discharge of artillery.

The engagement was soon over, without special results
beyond that *prestige* which we may be confident was, at
the moment, Jackson's main aim.   Before day he fell back
two miles, and in the narrowest part of the plain, some
four miles from town, began to make his permanent line
behind Rodriguez Canal.

Inclement weather set in, increasing the hardships of
friend and foe.   The British toiled incessantly in the
miry ground of the sugar-cane fields to bring up their

13

heavy artillery, and both sides erected breastworks and batteries, and hurried forward their re-enforcements. Skirmishing was frequent, and to Jackson's raw levies very valuable. Red-hot shot from the British works destroyed the *Carolina;* but her armament was saved and made a shore battery on the farther river bank. On New Year's day a few bales of cotton, forming part of the American fortifications, were scattered in all directions and set on fire, and this was the first and last use made of this material during the campaign. When it had been called to General Jackson's notice that this cotton was the property of a foreigner,—" Give him a gun and let him defend it," was his answer. On the 4th, two thousand two hundred and fifty Kentuckians, poorly clad and worse armed arrived, and such as bore serviceable weapons raised Jackson's force to three thousand two hundred men on his main line ; a line, says the Duke of Saxe-Weimar, " the very feeblest an engineer could have devised, that is, a straight one."

Yet on this line the defenders of New Orleans were about to be victorious. It consisted of half a mile of very uneven earthworks stretching across the plain along the inner edge of the canal, from the river to the edge of the wood, and continuing a like distance into the forest. In here it quickly dwindled to a mere double row of logs two feet apart, filled in between with earth. The entire artillery on this whole line was twelve pieces. But it was served by men of rare skill, artillerists of the regular army, the sailors of the burnt *Carolina*, some old French soldiers

under Flaujeac one of Bonaparte's gunners, and Dominique
and Beluche, with the tried cannoneers of their pirate ships.

From battery to battery the rude line was filled out
with a droll confusion of arms and trappings, men and
dress.   Here on the extreme right, just on and under
the levee, were some regular infantry and a company of
" Orleans Rifles," with some dragoons who served a how-

Jackson's Headquarters.

itzer.   Next to them was a battalion of Louisiana Creoles in gay and varied uniforms. The sailors of the *Carolina* were grouped around the battery between. In the
Creoles' midst were the swarthy privateers with their two
twenty-fours.   Then came a battalion of native men of
color, another bunch of sailors around a thirty-two-
pounder, a battalion of St. Domingan mulattoes, a stretch

of blue for some regular artillery and the Forty-fourth infantry, then Flaujeac and his Francs behind a brass twelve-pounder; next, a long slender line of brown homespun hunting-shirts that draped Carroll's lank Tennesseeans, then a small, bright bunch of marines, then some more regular artillery behind a long brass culverine and a six-pounder, then Adair's ragged Kentuckians, and at the end, Coffee's Tennesseeans, disappearing in the swamp, where they stood by day knee-deep in water and slept at night in the mud.

Wintry rains had retarded everything in the British camp, but at length Lambert's division came up, Packenham took command, and plans were perfected for the final attack. A narrow continuation of the canal by which the English had come up through the swamp to its head at the rear of Villeré's plantation was dug, so that their boats could be floated up to the river front close under the back of the levee, and then dragged over its top and launched into the river. The squalid negresses that fish for crawfish along its rank, flowery banks still call it, "Cannal Packin'am." All night of the 7th of January there came to the alert ears of the Americans across the intervening plain a noise of getting boats through this narrow passage. It was evident that the decisive battle was impending. Packenham's intention was to throw a considerable part of his force across the river to attack the effective marine battery abreast of the American line, erected there by Commodore Paterson,

while he, on the hither shore, unembarrassed by its fire
on his flank, should fall furiously upon Jackson's main
line, in three perpendicular columns.

But the river had fallen. Colonel Thornton, who was
to lead the movement on the farther bank, was long getting his boats across the levee. The current, too, was far
swifter than it had seemed. Eight priceless hours slipped
away and only a third of the intended force crossed.

Packenham's Headquarters (from the rear).

A little before daybreak of the 8th, the British main
force moved out of camp and spread across the plain, six
thousand strong, the Americans in front, the river on
their left, and the swamp-forest on their right. They had
planned to begin at one signal the three attacks on the
nearer and the one on the farther shore. The air was
chilly and obscure. A mist was slowly clearing off from
the wet and slippery ground. A dead silence reigned;
but in that mist and silence their enemy was waiting for

them. Presently day broke and rapidly brightened, the mist lifted a little and the red lines of the British were fitfully descried from the American works. Outside the levee the wide river and farther shore were quite hidden by the fog, which now and then floated hitherward over the land.

Packenham was listening for the attack of Colonel Thornton on the opposite bank, that was to relieve his main assault from the cross-fire of Paterson's marine battery. The sun rose; but he heard nothing. He waited till half-past seven; still there was no sound.

Meanwhile the Americans lay in their long trench, peering over their sorry breastworks, and wondering at the inaction. But at length Packenham could wait no longer. A British rocket went up near the swamp. It was the signal for attack. A single cannon-shot answered from the Americans, and the artillery on both sides opened with a frightful roar. On Jackson's extreme left, some black troops of the British force made a feint against the line in the swamp and were easily repulsed. On his right, near the river, the enemy charged in solid column, impetuously, upon a redoubt just in advance of the line. Twice only the redoubt could reply, and the British were over and inside and pressing on to scale the breastwork behind. Their brave and much-loved Colonel Rennie was leading them. But on the top of the works he fell dead with the hurrah on his lips, and they were driven back and out of the redoubt in confusion.

Meantime the main attack was being made in the open

plain near the edge of the swamp. Some four hundred yards in front of the American works lay a ditch. Here the English formed in close column of about sixty men front. They should have laid off their heavy knapsacks, for they were loaded besides with big fascines of ripe sugar-cane for filling up the American ditch, and with scaling ladders. But with muskets, knapsacks and all, they gave three cheers and advanced. Before them went a shower of Congreve rockets. For a time they were partly covered by an arm of the forest and by the fog, but soon they emerged from both and moved steadily forward in perfect order, literally led to the slaughter in the brave old British way.

"Where are you going?" asked one English officer of another.

"I'll be hanged if I know."

"Then," said the first, "you have got into what I call a good thing; a far-famed American battery is in front of you at a short range, and on the left of this spot is flanked, at eight hundred yards, by their batteries on the opposite side of the river."

"The first objects we saw, enclosed as it were in this little world of mist," says this eye-witness, "were the cannon-balls tearing up the ground and crossing one another, and bounding along like so many cricket-balls through the air, coming on our left flank from the American batteries on the right bank of the river, and also from their lines in front."

The musketry fire of the Americans, as well as the artillery, was given with terrible precision. Unhappily for the English they had singled out for their attack those homely-clad men whom they had nick-named the "Dirty-shirts,"—the riflemen of Kentucky and Tennessee—Indian fighters, that never fired but on a selected victim. Flaujeac's battery tore out whole files of men. Yet the brave foe came on, veterans from the Cape of Good Hope and from the Spanish Peninsula, firmly and measuredly, and a few platoons had even reached the canal, when the column faltered, gave way, and fled precipitately back to the ditch where it had first formed.

Here there was a rally. The knapsacks were taken off. Re-enforcements came up. The first charge had been a dreadful mistake in its lack of speed. Now the start was quicker and in less order, but again in the fatal columnar form.

"At a run," writes the participant already quoted, "we neared the American line. The mist was now rapidly clearing away, but, owing to the dense smoke, we could not at first distinguish the attacking column of the British troops to our right. . . . The echo from the cannonade and musketry was so tremendous in the forests that the vibration seemed as if the earth were cracking and tumbling to pieces. . . . The flashes of fire looked as if coming out of the bowels of the earth, so little above its surface were the batteries of the Americans."

Packenham led the van. On a black horse, in brilliant

uniform, waving his hat and cheering the onset, he was a mark the backwoodsmen could not miss. Soon he reeled and fell from his horse with a mortal wound; Gibbs followed him. Then Kean was struck and borne from the field with many others of high rank, and the column again recoiled and fell back, finally discomfited.

"Did you ever see such a scene?" cried one of Packenham's staff. "There is nothing left but the Seventh and Forty-third!"

The Battle-Ground.

"They fell," says another Englishman, "like the very blades of grass beneath the scythe of the mower. Seventeen hundred and eighty-one victims, including three generals, seven colonels, and seventy-five lesser officers, were the harvest of those few minutes."

At length the American musketry ceased. Only the batteries were answering shot for shot, when from the further side of the Mississippi came, all too late, a few reports of cannon, a short, brisk rattle of fire-arms, a hush, and three British cheers to tell that the few raw American troops on that side had been overpowered, and that Paterson's battery, prevented from defending itself by the blundering of the militia in its front, had been spiked and abandoned.

The batteries of the British line continued to fire until two in the afternoon; but from the first signal of the morning to the abandonment of all effort to storm the American works was but one hour, and the battle of New Orleans was over at half-past eight. General Lambert reported the British loss two thousand and seventeen; Jackson, the American at six killed and seven wounded.

From the 9th to the 18th four British vessels bombarded Fort St. Philip without result; on the morning of the 19th the British camp in front of Jackson was found deserted, and eight days later the last of the enemies' forces embarked from the shores of Lake Borgne.

The scenes of triumphant rejoicing, the hastily erected arches in the Place d'Armes, the symbolical impersonations, the myriads of banners and pennons, the columns of victorious troops, the crowded balconies, the rain of flowers in a town where flowers never fail, the huzzas of the thronging populace, the salvos of artillery, the garland-crowned victor, and the ceremonies of thanksgiving in the solemn cathedral, form a part that may be entrusted to the imagination. One purpose and one consummation made one people, and little of sorrow and naught of discord in that hour mingled with the joy of deliverance.

XXVIII.

THE END OF THE PIRATES.

NEW ORLEANS emerged from the smoke of battle comparatively Americanized. Peace followed, or rather the tardy news of peace, which had been sealed at Ghent more than a fortnight before the battle. With peace came open ports. The highways of commercial greatness crossed each other in the custom-house, not behind it as in Spanish or embargo days, and the Baratarians were no longer esteemed a public necessity. Scattered, used, and pardoned, they passed into eclipse—not total, but fatally dark where they most desired to shine. The ill-founded tradition that the Lafittes were never seen after the battle of New Orleans had thus a figurative reality.

In Jackson's general order of January 21st, Captains Dominique and Beluche, "with part of their former crew," were gratefully mentioned for their gallantry in the field, and the brothers Lafitte for "the same courage and fidelity." On these laurels Dominique You rested and settled down to quiet life in New Orleans, enjoying the vulgar admiration which is given to the survivor of lawless adventures. It may seem superfluous to add that he became a leader in ward politics.

In the spring of 1815, Jackson, for certain imprisonments of men who boldly opposed the severity of his prolonged dictatorship in New Orleans, was forced at length

Old Spanish Cottage in Royal Street, Scene of Andrew Jackson's Trial.

to regard the decrees of court. It was then that the "hellish banditti," turned "Jacksonites," did their last swaggering in the famous Exchange Coffee-house, at the corner of St. Louis and Chartres Streets, and when he was fined $1,000 for contempt of court, aided in drawing his carriage by hand through the streets.

Of Beluche or of Pierre Lafitte little or nothing more is known. But John Lafitte continued to have a record. After the city's deliverance a ball was given to officers of the army. General Coffee was present. So, too, was Lafitte. On their being brought together and introduced, the General showed some hesitation of manner, whereupon the testy Baratarian advanced haughtily and said, with emphasis, "Lafitte, the pirate." Thus, unconsciously, it may be, he foretold that part of his life which still lay in the future.

That future belongs properly to the history of Texas. Galveston Island had early been one of Lafitte's stations, and now became his permanent depôt, whence he carried on extensive operations, contraband and piratical. His principal cruiser was the *Jupiter*. She sailed under a Texan commission. Under the filibuster Long, who ruled at Nacogdoches, Lafitte became Governor of Galveston.

An American ship was robbed of a quantity of specie on the high seas. Shortly afterward the *Jupiter* came into Galveston with a similar quantity on board. A United States cruiser accordingly was sent to lay off the coast, and watch her manœuvres. Lafitte took offence at this, and sent to the American commander to demand explanation. His letter, marked with more haughtiness, as well as with more ill-concealed cunning than his earlier correspondence with the British and Americans, was not answered.

In 1818 a storm destroyed four of his fleet. He sent

one Lafage to New Orleans, who brought out thence a new schooner of two guns, manned by fifty men. He presently took a prize; but had hardly done so, when he was met by the revenue cutter *Alabama*, answered her challenge with a broadside, engaged her in a hard battle, and only surrendered after heavy loss. The schooner and prize were carried into Bayou St. John, the crew taken to New Orleans, tried in the United States Court, condemned and executed.

Once more Lafitte took the disguise of a Colombian commission and fitted out three vessels. The name of one is not known. Another was the *General Victoria*, and a third the schooner *Blank*—or, we may venture to spell it *Blanque*. He coasted westward and southward as far as Sisal, Yucatan, taking several small prizes, and one that was very valuable, a schooner that had been a slaver. Thence he turned toward Cape Antonio, Cuba, and in the open Gulf disclosed to his followers that his Colombian commission had expired.

Forty-one men insisted on leaving him. He removed the guns of the *General Victoria*, crippled her rigging, and gave her into their hands. They sailed for the Mississippi, and after three weeks arrived there and surrendered to the officers of the customs. The Spanish Consul claimed the vessel, but she was decided to belong to the men who had fitted her out.

Lafitte seems now to have become an open pirate. Villeré, Governor of Louisiana after Claiborne, and the same

who had counselled the acceptance of Lafitte's first overtures in 1819, spoke in no measured terms of "those men
who lately, under the false pretext of serving the cause of
the Spanish patriots, scoured the Gulf of Mexico, making
its waves groan," etc.   It seems many of them had found
homes in New Orleans, making it "the seat of disorders
and crimes which he would not attempt to describe."

The end of this uncommon man is lost in a confusion
of improbable traditions. As late as 1822 his name, if not
his person, was the terror of the Gulf and the Straits of
Florida.   But in that year the United States Navy swept
those waters with vigor, and presently reduced the perils
of the Gulf—for the first time in its history—to the
hazard of wind and wave.

A few steps down the central walk of the middle cemetery of those that lie along Claiborne Street from Custom-
house down to Conti, on the right-hand side, stands the
low, stuccoed tomb of Dominique You.   The tablet bears
his name surmounted by the emblem of Free Masonry.
Some one takes good care of it.   An epitaph below pro-
claims him, in French verse, the "intrepid hero of a hundred battles on land and sea; who, without fear and without reproach, will one day view, unmoved, the destruction
of the world."   To this spot, in 1830, he was followed on
his way by the Louisiana Legion (city militia), and laid to
rest with military honors, at the expense of the town
council.

Governor Claiborne left the executive chair in 1816 to

represent the State in the United States Senate. His successor was a Creole, the son, as we have seen, of that fiery
Villeré who in 1769 had died in Spanish captivity one of
the very earliest martyrs to the spirit of American free-

Tomb of Governor Claiborne's Family.
[*From a Photograph.*]

dom. Claiborne did not live out the year, but in the winter died. In the extreme rear of the old St. Louis cemetery on Basin Street, New Orleans, in an angle of its high
brick wall, shut off from the rest of the place by a rude,
low fence of cypress palisades, is a narrow piece of uncon-

secrated ground where the tombs of some of New Orleans' noblest dead are huddled together in miserable oblivion. Rank weeds and poisonous vines have so choked up the whole place, that there is no way for the foot but over the tops of the tombs, and one who ventures thus, must beware of snakes at every step. In the midst of this spot is the tomb of Eliza Washington Claiborne, the Governor's first wife, of her child of three years who died the same day as she, and of his secretary, her brother, of twenty-five, who a few months later fell in a duel, the rash victim of insults heaped upon his sister's husband through the public press. Near by, just within the picketed enclosure, the sexton has been for years making a heap of all manner of grave-yard rubbish, and under that pile of old coffin planks, broken-glass, and crockery, tincans, and rotting evergreens, lie the tomb and the ashes of William Charles Cole Claiborne, Governor of Louisiana.

14

XXIX.

FAUBOURG STE. MARIE.

IF one will stand to-day on the broad levee at New Orleans, with his back to the Mississippi, a short way
out to the left and riverward from the spot where the long-
vanished little Fort St. Louis once made pretence of guard-
ing the town's upper river corner, he will look down two
streets at once. They are Canal and Common, which
gently diverge from their starting-point at his feet and
narrow away before his eye as they run down toward the
low, unsettled lots and commons behind the city.

Canal Street, the centre and pride of New Orleans, takes
its name from the slimy old moat that once festered under
the palisade wall of the Spanish town, where it ran back
from river to swamp and turned northward on the line
now marked by the beautiful tree-planted Rampart Street.

Common Street marks the ancient boundary of the es-
tates wrested from the exiled Jesuit fathers by confisca-
tion. In the beginning of the present century, the long
wedge-shaped tract between these two lines was a Government reservation, kept for the better efficiency of the fortifications that overlooked its lower border and for a

public road to No-man's land. It was called the Terre Commune.

That part of the Jesuits' former plantations that lay next to the Terre Commune was mainly the property of a singular personage named Jean Gravier. Its farther-side boundary was on a line now indicated by Delord Street. When the fire of 1788 laid nearly the half of New Orleans in ashes, his father, Bertrand, and his mother, Marie, had laid off this tract into lots and streets, to the depth of three squares backward from the river, and called it Villa Gravier. On her death, the name was changed in her honor, and so became the Faubourg Ste. Marie.

Capitalists had smiled upon the adventure. Julian Poydras, Claude Girod, Julia a free woman of color, and others had given names to its cross-streets by buying corner-lots on its river-front. Along this front, under the breezy levee, ran the sunny and dusty Tchoupitoulas road, entering the town's southern river-side gate, where a sentry-box and Spanish corporal's guard drowsed in the scant shadow of Fort St. Louis. Outside the levee the deep Mississippi glided, turbid, silent, often overbrimming, with many a swirl and upward heave of its boiling depths, and turning, sent a long smooth eddy back along this " making bank," while its main current hurried onward, townward, *northward*, as if it would double on invisible pursuers before it swept to the east and southeast from the Place d'Armes and disappeared behind the low groves of Slaughterhouse Point.

In the opening years of the century only an occasional villa and an isolated roadside shop or two had arisen along the front of Faubourg Ste. Marie and in the first street behind. *Calle del Almazen*, the Spanish notary wrote this street's name, for its lower (northern) end looked across the Terre Commune upon the large Almazen or store-house of Kentucky tobacco which Don Estevan Miró thought it wise to keep filled with purchases from the perfidious Wilkinson. Rue du Magasin, Storehouse Street, the Creoles translated it, and the Americans made it Magazine Street ; but it was still only a straight road. Truck-gardens covered the fertile arpents between and beyond. Here and there was a grove of wide-spreading live-oaks, here and there a clump of persimmon trees, here and there an orchard of figs, here and there an avenue of bitter oranges or of towering pecans. The present site of the " St. Charles " was a cabbage-garden. Midway between Poydras and Girod Streets, behind Magazine, lay a *campo de negros*, a slave camp, probably of cargoes of Guinea or Congo slaves. The street that cut through it became Calle del Campo—Camp Street.

Far back in the rear of these lands, on the old Poydras draining canal, long since filled up and built upon—in a lonely, dreary waste of weeds and bushes dotted thick with cypress stumps and dwarf palmetto, full of rankling ponds choked with bulrushes, flags, and pickerel-weed, fringed by willows and reeds, and haunted by frogs, snakes, crawfish, rats, and mosquitoes, on the edge of the tangled swamp forest—stood the dilapidated home of "Doctor" Gravier. It stood on high pillars. Its windows and doors were lofty and wide, its verandas were broad, its roof was steep, its chimneys were tall, and its occupant was a childless, wifeless, companionless old man, whose kindness and medical attention to negroes had won him his professional title. He claims mention as a type of that strange group of men which at this early period figured here as the shrewd acquirers of wide suburban tracts, leaders of lonely lives, and leavers of great fortunes.

John McDonough, who at this time was a young man, a thrifty trader in Guinea negroes, and a suitor for the hand of Don Andreas Almonaster's fair daughter, the late Baroness Pontalba, became in after days a like solitary type of the same class. Jean Gravier's house long survived him, a rendezvous for desperate characters, and, if rumor is correct, the scene of many a terrible murder.

In the favoring eddy under the river-bank in front of Faubourg Ste. Marie landed the flat-boat fleets from the Ohio, the Tennessee, and the Cumberland. Buyers crowded here for cheap and fresh provisions. The huge, huddled arks became a floating market-place, with the kersey- and woolsey- and jeans-clad bargemen there, and the Creole and his sometimes brightly clad and sometimes picturesquely ragged slave here, and the produce of the West changing hands between. But there was more than this. Warehouses began to appear on the edge of Tchoupitoulas road, and barrels of pork and flour and meal to run bickering down into their open doors from the levee's top. Any eye could see that, only let war cease, there would be a wonderful change in the half-drained, sun-baked marshes and kitchen-gardens of Faubourg Ste. Marie.

Presently the change came. It outran the official news of peace. " Our harbor," wrote Claiborne, the Governor, in March, 1815, " is again whitening with canvas; the levee is crowded with cotton, tobacco, and other articles for exportation."

A full sunrise of prosperity shone upon New Orleans. The whole great valley above began to fill up with wonderful speed and to pour down into her lap the fruits of its agriculture. Thirty-three thousand people were astir in her homes and streets. They overran the old bounds. They pulled up the old palisade. They shovelled the earthworks into the moat and pushed their streets out into the fields and thickets. In the old narrow ways—and the wider new ones alike—halls, churches, schools, stores, warehouses, banks, hotels, and theatres sprang up by day and night.

Faubourg Ste. Marie outstripped all other quarters. The unconservative American was everywhere, but in Faubourg Ste. Marie he was supreme. The Western trade crowded down like a breaking up of ice. In 1817, 1,500 flat-boats and 500 barges tied up to the willows of the levee before the new faubourg. Inflation set in. Exports ran up to thirteen million dollars' worth.

In 1819 came the collapse, but development overrode it. Large areas of the *batture* were reclaimed in front of the faubourg, and the Americans covered them with store buildings. In 1812, the first steam vessel had come down the Mississippi; in 1816, for the first time, one overcame and reascended its current; in 1821, 441 flat-boats and 174 barges came to port, and there were 287 arrivals of steam-boats.

The kitchen-gardens vanished. Gravier Street, between Tchoupitoulas and Magazine, was paved with cobble-stones. The Creoles laughed outright. " A stone pave-ment in New Orleans soil ? It will sink out of sight ! " But it bore not only their ridicule, but an uproar and gorge of wagons and drays. There was an avalanche of trade. It crammed the whole harbor-front—old town and new—with river and ocean fleets. It choked the streets. The cry was for room and facilities. The Creoles heeded it. Up came their wooden sidewalks and curbs, brick and stone went down in their place, and by 1822 gangs of street paviors were seen and heard here, there, and yonder, swinging the pick and ramming the roundstone. There were then 41,000 people in the town and its suburbs.

The old population held its breath. It clung bravely to the failing trades of the West Indies, France, and Spain. Coffee, indigo, sugar, rice, and foreign fruits and wines were still handled in the Rues Toulouse, Conti, St. Louis, Chartres, St. Peter, and Royale; but the lion's share— the cotton, the tobacco, pork, beef, corn, flour, and north-

ern and British fabrics—poured into and out of Faubourg
Ste. Marie through the hands of the swarming Americans.

"New Orleans is going to be a mighty city," said they
in effect, "and we are going to be New Orleans." But
the Creole was still powerful, and jealous of everything
that hinted of American absorption. We have seen that,
in 1816, he elected one of his own race, General Villeré, to
succeed Claiborne in the governor's chair, and to guard the
rights that headlong Americans might forget. "Indeed,"
this governor wrote in a special message on the "scandalous practices almost every instant taking place in New
Orleans and its suburbs"—"Indeed, we should be cautious
in receiving all foreigners." That caution was of little
avail.

XXX.

WHAT a change! The same Governor Villeré could not but say, "The Louisianian who retraces the condition of his country under the government of kings can never cease to bless the day when the great American confederation received him into its bosom." It was easy for Louisianians to be Americans; but to let Americans be Louisianians!—there was the rub. Yet it had to be. In ten years, the simple export and import trade of the port had increased fourfold; and in the face of inundations and pestilences, discord of sentiment and tongues, and the saddest of public morals and disorder, the population had nearly doubled.

Nothing could stop the inflow of people and wealth. In the next ten years, 1820–30, trade increased to one and three-quarters its already astonishing volume. The inhabitants were nearly 50,000, and the strangers from all parts of America and the commercial world were a small army. Sometimes there would be five or six thousand up-river bargemen in town at once, wild, restless, and unemployed. On the levee especially this new tremendous life and energy heaved and palpitated. Between 1831 and 1835, the mere foreign exports and imports ran up from twenty-six to nearly fifty-four million dollars. There were no wharves built out into the harbor yet, and all the vast mass of produce and goods lay out under the open sky on the long, wide, unbroken level of the curving harbor-front where Ohio bargemen, Germans, Mississippi raftsmen, Irishmen, French, English, Creoles, Yankees, and negro and mulatto slaves surged and jostled and filled the air with shouts and imprecations.

Vice put on the same activity that commerce showed. The Creole had never been a strong moral force. The American came in as to gold diggings or diamond fields, to grab and run. The transatlantic immigrant of those days was frequently the offscouring of Europe. The West Indian was a leader in licentiousness, gambling and duelling. The number of billiard-rooms, gaming-houses, and lottery-offices was immense. In the old town they seemed to be every second house. There was the French Evangelical Church Lottery, the Baton Rouge Church Lottery, the Natchitoches Catholic Church Lottery, and a host of others less piously inclined. The cafés of the central town were full of filibusters. In 1819, "General" Long sailed hence against Galveston. In 1822, a hundred and fifty men left New Orleans in the sloop-of-war *Eureka*, and assisted in the taking of Porto Cabello, Venezuela. The paving movement had been only a flurry or two, and even in the heart of the town, where carriages sometimes sank to their axles in mud, highway robbery and murder lay always in wait for the incautious night wayfarer who ventured out alone. The police was a mounted *gendarmerie* If the Legislature committed a tenth of the wickedness it was charged with, it was sadly corrupt. The worst day of all the week was Sunday. The stores and shops were open, but toil slackened and license gained headway. Gambling-rooms and ball-rooms were full, weapons were often out, the quadroon masques of the Salle de Condé were thronged with men of high standing, and crowds of barge and raftsmen, as well as Creoles and St. Domingans, gathered at those open-air African dances, carousals, and debaucheries in the rear of the town that have left their monument in the name of "Congo" Square.

Yet still prosperity smiled and commerce roared along the streets of the town and her faubourgs—Ste. Marie on her right, Marigny on her left—with ever-rising volume and value, and in spite of fearful drawbacks. The climate was deadly to Americans, and more deadly to the squalid immigrant. Social life, unattractive at best, received the Creole and shut the door. The main town was without beauty, and the landscape almost without a dry foothold. Schools were scarce and poor, churches few and ill attended, and domestic service squalid, inefficient, and corrupt. Between 1810 and 1837 there were fifteen epidemics of yellow fever. Small-pox was frequent. In 1832, while yellow fever was still epidemic, cholera entered and carried off one person in every six; many of the dead were buried where they died, and many were thrown into the river. Moreover, to get to the town or to leave it was a journey famed for its dangers. On one steamboat, three hundred lives were lost; on another, one hundred and thirty; on another, the same number; on another, one hundred and twenty. The cost of running a steamer was six times as great as on the northern lakes.

Without these drawbacks what would New Orleans have been? For, with them all, and with others which we pass by, her population between 1830 and 1840 once more doubled its numbers. She was the fourth city of the United States in the number of her people. Cincinnati, which in the previous decade had outgrown her, was surpassed and distanced. Only New York, Philadelphia, and Baltimore were larger. Boston was nearly as large; but besides these there was no other city in the Union of half her numbers. Faubourg Ste. Marie had swallowed up the suburbs above her until it comprised the whole expanse of the old Jesuits' plantations to the line of Felicity Road. The old Marquis Marigny de Mandeville, whose plantation lay on the lower edge of the town just across the Esplanade, had turned it into lots and streets, and the town had run over upon it and covered it with small residences, and here and there a villa. The city boundaries had been extended to take in both these faubourgs; and the three " municipalities," as they were called, together numbered one hundred and two thousand inhabitants.

The ends of the harbor front were losing sight of each

other. In the seasons of high water the tall, broad, frail-looking steamers that crowded in together, " bow on," at the busy levee, hidden to their hurricane roofs in cargoes

Old Bourse and St. Louis Hotel. (Afterward the State House).

of cotton bales, looked down upon not merely a quiet little Spanish-American town of narrow streets, low, heavy, rugged roofs, and Latin richness and variety of color peeping out of a mass of overshadowing greenery. Fort St.

Charles, the last fraction of the old fortifications, was gone, and the lofty chimney of a United States mint smoked in its place. The new Bourse, later known as St. Louis Hotel, and yet later as the famed State-house of Reconstruction days, just raised its low, black dome into view above the intervening piles of brick. A huge prison lifted its frowning walls and quaint Spanish twin belfries gloomily over Congo Square. At the white-stuccoed Merchants' Exchange, just inside the old boundary on the Canal Street side, a stream of men poured in and out, for there was the Post-office. Down in the lower arm of the river's bend shone the Third Municipality,—which had been Faubourg Marigny. On its front, behind a net-work of shipping, stood the Levee Cotton Press; it had cost half a million dollars. Here on the south, sweeping far around and beyond the view almost to the "Bull's Head Coffeehouse," was the Second Municipality, once Faubourg Ste. Marie, with its lines and lines of warehouses, its Orleans Press, that must needs cost a quarter million more than the other, and many a lesser one. The town was full of banks : the Commercial, the Atchafalaya, the Orleans, the Canal, the City, etc. Banks's Arcade was there, a glass-roofed mercantile court in the midst of a large hotel in Magazine Street, now long known as the St. James. Hotels were numerous. In Camp and St. Charles Streets stood two theatres, where the world's stars deigned to present themselves, and the practical jokers of the upper galleries concocted sham fights and threw straw men over into the pit below, with cries of murder. Here and there a church—the First Presbyterian, the Carondelet Methodist—raised an admonitory finger. The site of old Jean Gravier's house was hidden behind Poydras Market; the

uncanny iron frames of the Gas Works rose beyond. The reservoir of the water-works lay in here to the left near the river, whose muddy water it used. Back yonder in the street named for Julia, the f. w. c.,* a little bunch of schooner masts and pennons showed where the Canal Bank had dug a "New Basin" and brought the waters of Lake Pontchartrain up into this part of the city also.

It was the period when the American idea of architect-

---

* "Free woman of color"—initials used in the Louisiana courts and notarial documents.

ure had passed from its untrained innocence to a sopho-
moric affectation of Greek forms. Banks, hotels, churches,
theatres, mansions, cottages, all were Ionic or Corinthian,
and the whole American quarter was a gleaming white.
But the commercial shadow of this quarter fell darkly upon
the First Municipality, the old town. A quiet crept into
the Rue Toulouse. The fashionable shops on the Rue
Royale slipped away and spread out in Canal Street. The
vault of the St. Louis dome still echoed the voice of the
double-tongued, French-English auctioneer of town lots
and slaves; but in the cabbage-garden of " old Mr.
Percy," in the heart of Faubourg Ste. Marie, a resplendent rival, the palatial St. Charles, lifted its dazzling
cupola high above all surroundings and overpeered old
town and new, river, plain, and receding forest. Its rotunda was the unofficial guildhall of all the city's most
active elements. Here met the capitalist, the real estate
operator, the merchant, the soldier, the tourist, the politi-
cian, the filibuster, the convivialist, the steamboat captain,
the horse-fancier; and ever conspicuous among the throng
—which had a trick of separating suddenly and dodging
behind the pillars of the rotunda at the sound of high
words—was a man, a type, an index of great wealth to
New Orleans, who in this spot was never a stranger and
was never quite at home.

The Picayune Tier.

XXXI.

FLUSH TIMES.

THE brow and cheek of this man were darkened by outdoor exposure, but they were not weather-beaten. His shapely, bronzed hand was no harder or rougher than was due to the use of the bridle-rein and the gunstock. His eye was the eye of a steed; his neck—the same. His hair was a little luxuriant. His speech was positive, his manner was military, his sentiments were antique, his clothing was of broadcloth, his boots were neat, and his hat was soft, broad, and slouched a little to show its fineness. Such in his best aspect was the Mississippi River planter. When sugar was his crop and Creole French his native tongue, his polish would sometimes be finer still, with a finish got in Paris, and his hotel would be the St. Louis.

He was growing to be a great power. The enormous agricultural resources of Louisiana, Mississippi, Arkansas, and Tennessee were his. The money-lender gyrated around him with sweet smiles and open purse. He was mortgaged to the eyes, and still commanded a credit that courted and importuned him. He caused an immense increase of trade. His extravagant wants and the needs

of his armies of slaves kept the city drained of its capital
almost or quite the whole year round.   Borrower and
lender vied with each other in recklessness.   Much the
larger portion of all the varied products of the West received in New Orleans was reshipped, not to sea, but to
the plantations of the interior, often returning along the
same route half the distance they had originally come.
Millions of capital that would have yielded slower but
immensely better final results in other channels went into
the planters' paper, based on the value of slaves and of
lands whose value depended on slave labor,—a species of
wealth unexchangeable in the great world of commerce,
fictitious as paper money, and even more illusory.   But,
like the paper money that was then inundating the country, this system produced an immense volume of business;
and this, in turn, called into the city, to fill the streets and
landings and the thousands of humble dwellings that
sprang up throughout the old Faubourg Marigny and
spread out on the right flank of Faubourg Ste. Marie, the
Irish and German emigrant, by tens of thousands.

It was in the midst of these conditions that mad specu-
lations in Western lands and the downfall of the United
States Bank rolled the great financial crisis of 1837 across
the continent.   Where large results had intoxicated enterprise, banks without number, and often without foundation, strewed their notes among the infatuated people.
But in New Orleans enterprise had forgotten everything
but the factorage of the staple crops.   The banks were

A Cotton Press and Yard.

not so many, but they followed the fashion in having make-believe capital and in crumbling to ashes at a touch. Sixty millions of capital, four of deposits, twelve hundred thousand specie, eighteen hundred thousand real estate, and seventy-two millions receivables, mostly protested,—such was their record when they suspended.

"A whirlwind of ruin," said one of the newspapers, "prostrated the greater portion of the city." Everybody's hands were full of "shin-plasters." There was no other currency. Banks and banking were execrated, and their true office so ill understood that a law was passed preventing the establishment of any such institution in the State. A few old banks that weathered the long financial stress accepted, with silent modesty, the monopoly thus thrown into their hands, and in 1843, having abandoned the weaker concerns to shipwreck, resumed specie payment. The city's foreign commerce had dropped to thirty-four and three-quarters million dollars, a loss of nineteen millions; but, for the first time in her history, she sent to sea a million bales of cotton.

The crisis had set only a momentary check upon agriculture. The financiers of New Orleans came out of it more than ever infatuated with the plantation idea. It had become the ruling principle in the social organism of the South, the one tremendous drawback to the best development of country and city; and now the whole lower Mississippi Valley threw all its energies and all its fortune into this seductive mistake.

And still the city grew; grew as the Delta sands on which it stands had grown, by the compulsory tribute of the Mississippi. The great staples of the Valley poured down ever more and more. In 1842, the value of these receipts was $45,700,000; in 1844, it was $60,000,000; in 1846, it was over $77,000,000; in 1847, it was $90,000,000; in 1850, it was close to $97,000,000. The city lengthened; it broadened; it lifted its head higher. The trowel rang everywhere on home-made brick and imported granite, and houses rose by hundreds. The Irish and Germans thronged down from the decks of emigrant ships at the rate of thirty thousand a year. They even partly crowded out slave service. In 1850, there were 5,330 slaves less in the city than in 1840. The free mulatto also gave way. Unenterprising, despised, persecuted, this caste, once so scant in numbers, had grown, in 1840, to be nearly as numerous as the whites. The " abolition " question brought them double hatred and suspicion ; and restrictive, unjust, and intolerant State legislation reduced their numbers— it must have been by exodus—from 19,000 to less than 10,000 souls. Allowing for natural increase, eleven or twelve thousand must have left the city. The proportion of whites rose from fifty-eight to seventy-eight per cent., and the whole population of New Orleans and its environs was 133,650.

Another city had sprung up on the city's upper boundary. In 1833, three suburbs, Lafayette, Livaudais, and Réligeuses, the last occupying an old plantation of the

Ursuline nuns, combined into a town. About 1840, the
wealthy Americans began to move up here into "large,

Entrance to a Cotton Yard.

commodious, one-story houses, full of windows on all
sides, and surrounded by broad and shady gardens."

Here, but nearer the river, Germans and Irish—especially the former—filed in continually, and by 1850 the town of Lafayette contained over fourteen thousand residents, nearly all white.

It was a red-letter year. The first street pavement of large, square granite blocks was laid. Wharf building set in strongly. The wires of the electro-magnetic telegraph drew the city into closer connection with civilization. The mind of the financier was aroused, and he turned his eye toward railroads. The " Tehuantepec route" received its first decided impulse. Mexican grants were bought; surveys were procured ; much effort was made—and lost. The Mexican Government was too unstable and too fickle to be bargained with. But in 1851, meantime, two great improvements were actually set on foot; to wit, the two railways that eventually united the city with the great central system of the Union in the Mississippi-Ohio Valley, and with the vast Southwest, Mexico, and California. These two works moved slowly, but by 1855 and 1857 the railway trains were skimming out across the flowery *prairies tremblantes* eighty miles westward toward Texas, and the same distance northward toward the centre of the continent. In 1852, Lafayette and the municipalities were consolidated into one city government. Sixteen years of subdivision under separate municipal councils, and similar expensive and obstructive nonsense, had taught Creole, American, and immigrant the value of unity and of the American principles of growth better than unity could

have done it. Algiers, a suburb of machine shops and
nautical repair yards, began to grow conspicuous on the
farther side of the river.

The consolidation was a great step. The American
quarter became the centre and core of the whole city. Its
new and excessively classic marble municipality hall became the city hall. Its public grounds became the chosen
rendezvous of all popular assemblies. All the great trades
sought domicile in its streets; and the St. Charles, at
whose memorable burning, in 1850, the people wept, being
restored in 1852–53, made final eclipse of the old St.
Louis.

A small steel-engraved picture of New Orleans, made
just before this period, is obviously the inspiration of the
commercial and self-important American. The ancient
plaza, the cathedral, the old hall of the cabildo, the calaboza, the old Spanish barracks, the emptied convent of
the Ursulines, the antiquated and decayed Rue Toulouse,
the still quietly busy Chartres and Old Levee Streets—all
that was time-honored and venerable, are pushed out of
view, and the lately humble Faubourg Ste. Marie fills the
picture almost from side to side. Long ranks of huge,
lofty-chimneyed Mississippi steamers smoke at the levee;
and high above the deep and solid phalanxes of brick and
stone rise the majestic dome of the first St. Charles
and the stately tower of St. Patrick's Church, queen and
bishop of the board.

But the ancient landmarks trembled to a worse fate than

being left out of a picture. Renovation came in. In
1850, the cathedral was torn down to its foundations, and
began to rise again with all of its Spanish picturesqueness
lost and little or nothing gained in beauty. On its right
and left absurd French roofs were clapped upon the cabildo and the court-house. Old Don Andreas's daughter,
the Baroness Pontalba, replaced the quaint tile-roofed
store buildings that her father had built on either side of
the square with large, new rows of red brick. The city
laid out the Place d'Armes, once her grassy play-ground,
in blinding white-shell walks, trimmed shrubbery, and
dusty flower-beds, and later, in 1855, placed in its centre
the bronze equestrian figure of the deliverer of New
Orleans, and called the classic spot Jackson Square. Yet,
even so, it remains to the present the last lurking-place of
the romance of primitive New Orleans.

It was not a time to look for very good taste. All
thoughts were led away by the golden charms of commerce. In 1851, the value of receipts from the interior
was nearly $107,000,000. The mint coined $10,000,000,
mostly the product of California's new-found treasure-
fields. The year 1853 brought still greater increase. Of
cotton alone, there came sixty-eight and a quarter million
dollars' worth. The sugar crop was tens of thousands of
hogsheads larger than ever before. Over a tenth of all
the arrivals from sea were of steamships. There was
another inflation. Leaving out the immense unascertained
amounts of shipments *into* the interior, the city's business,

The Old Bank in Toulouse Street.

in 1856, rose to two hundred and seventy-one and a quarter millions. In 1857 it was three hundred and two millions. In this year came a crash, which the whole country felt. New Orleans felt it rather less than other cities, and quickly recovered.

We pause at 1860. In that year New Orleans rose to a prouder commercial exaltation than she had ever before enjoyed, and at its close began that sudden and swift descent which is not the least pathetic episode of our unfortunate civil war. In that year, the city that a hundred and forty years before had consisted of a hundred bark and palmetto-thatched huts in a noisome swamp counted, as the fraction of its commerce comprised in its exports, imports, and domestic receipts, the value of three hundred and twenty-four million dollars.

XXXII.

WHY NOT BIGGER THAN LONDON.

THE great Creole city's geographical position has always dazzled every eye except the cold, coy scrutiny of capital. "The position of New Orleans," said President Jefferson in 1804, "certainly destines it to be the greatest city the world has ever seen." He excepted neither Rome nor Babylon. But man's most positive predictions are based upon contingencies; one unforeseen victory over nature bowls them down; the seeming certainties of to-morrow are changed to the opposite certainties of to-day; deserts become gardens, gardens cities, and older cities the haunts of bats and foxes.

When the early Kentuckian and Ohioan accepted nature's highway to market, and proposed the conquest of New Orleans in order to lay that highway open, they honestly believed there was no other possible outlet to the commercial world. When steam navigation came, they hailed it with joy and without question. To them it seemed an ultimate result. To the real-estate hoarding Creole, to the American merchant who was crowding and chafing him, to every superficial eye at least, it seemed a pledge of unlimited commercial empire bestowed by the laws of gravitation.   Few saw in it the stepping-stone from the old system of commerce by natural highways to a new system by direct and artificial lines.

It is hard to understand, looking back from the present, how so extravagant a mistake could have been made by wise minds.   From the first—or perhaps, we should say, from the peace of 1815—the development of the West declined to wait on New Orleans, or even on steam.   In 1825, the new principle of commercial transportation— that despises alike the aid and the interference of nature —opened, at Buffalo, the western end of the Erie Canal, the gate-way of a new freight route to northern Atlantic tide-waters, many hundreds of leagues more direct than the long journey down the Mississippi to New Orleans and around the dangerous capes of Florida.   In the same year another canal was begun, and in 1832 it connected the Ohio with Lake Erie; so that, in 1835, the State of Ohio alone sent through Buffalo to Atlantic ports 86,000 barrels of flour, 98,000 bushels of wheat, and 2,500,000 staves.

Another outlet was found, better than all transits— manufactures.   Steam, driving all manner of machinery, built towns and cities.   Cincinnati had, in 1820, 32,000 inhabitants; in 1830, 52,000.   Pittsburg became, "in the extent of its manufactures, the only rival of Cincinnati in the West."   St. Louis, still in embryo, rose from 10,000 to 14,000.   Buffalo, a town of 2,100, quadrupled its numbers.

16

Meanwhile, far down in New Orleans the Creole, grimly, and the American, more boastfully, rejoiced in a blaze of prosperity that blinded both. How should they, in a rain of wealth, take note that, to keep pace with the wonderful development in the great valley above, their increase should have been three times as great as it was, and that the sun of illimitable empire, which had promised to shine brightest upon them, was shedding brighter promises and kinder rays eastward, and even northward, *across* nature's highways and barriers. Even steam navigation began, on the great lakes, to demonstrate that the golden tolls of the Mississippi were not all to be collected at one or even two gates.

How might this have been stopped? By no means. The moment East and West saw that straighter courses toward commercial Europe could be taken than wild nature offered, the direct became the natural route, and the circuitous the unnatural. East-and-west trade lines, meant, sooner or later, the commercial subordination of New Orleans, until such time as the growth of countries behind her in the Southwest should bring her also upon an east-and-west line. Meantime the new system could be delayed by improving the old, many of whose drawbacks were removable. That which could not be stopped could yet be postponed.

But there was one drawback that riveted all the rest. Through slave-holding, and the easy fortune-getting it afforded, an intellectual indolence spread everywhere, and

Among the Markets.

the merchant of Faubourg Ste. Marie, American—often New Englander—as he was, sank under the seductions of a livelihood so simple, so purely executive, and so rich in perquisites, as the marketing of raw crops. From this mental inertia sprang an invincible provincialism; the Creole, whose society he was always courting, intensified it. Better civilizations were too far away to disturb it. A "peculiar institution" doubled that remoteness, and an enervating, luxurious climate folded it again upon itself. It colored his financial convictions and all his conduct of public affairs. He confronted obstacles with serene apathy; boasted of his city's natural advantages, forgetting that it was man, not nature, that he had to contend with; surrendered ground which he might have held for generations; and smilingly ignored the fact that, with all her increase of wealth and population, his town was slipping back along the comparative scale of American cities. "Was she not the greatest in exports after New York?"

The same influence that made the Creole always and only a sugar, tobacco, or cotton factor, waived away the classes which might have brought in manufactures with them. Its shadow fell as a blight upon intelligent, trained labor. Immigrants from the British Isles and from Europe poured in; but those adepts in the mechanical and productive arts that so rapidly augment the fortunes of a commonwealth staid away; there was nothing in surrounding nature or society to evolve the operative from the hod-carrier and drayman, and the prospecting manufacturer and

his capital turned aside to newer towns where labor was
uncontemned, and skill and technical knowledge sprang
forward at the call of enlightened enterprise.

Men never guessed the whole money value of time until
the great inventions for the facilitation of commerce began
to appear. " Adopt us," these seemed to say as they came
forward in procession, " or you cannot become or even remain great." But, even so, only those cities lying somewhere on right lines between the great centres of supply
and demand could seize and hold them. It was the fate,
not the fault, of New Orleans not to be one such. St.
Louis, Louisville, Cincinnati, Pittsburg, Boston, New
York, Philadelphia, Baltimore, were more fortunate ;
while Cleveland, Buffalo, Chicago, were born of these new
conditions. The locomotive engine smote the commercial
domain of New Orleans in half, and divided the best part
of her trade beyond the mouth of the Ohio among her
rivals. In that decade of development—1830-40—when
the plantation idea was enriching her with one hand and
robbing her of double with the other, the West was filling
with town life, and railroads and canals were starting
eagerly eastward and westward, bearing immense burdens
of freight and travel, and changing the scale of miles to
that of minutes. Boston and New York had pre-empted
the future with their daring outlays, and clasped hands
tighter with the States along the Ohio by lines of direct
transit. Pennsylvania joined Philadelphia with the same
river, and spent more money in railroads and canals than

Exchange Alley. (Old Passage de la Bourse.) Looking toward the American Quarter.

any other State in the Union. Baltimore reached out her Chesapeake & Ohio canal and railway. Ohio and Indiana spent millions. But the census of 1840 proclaimed New Orleans the fourth city of the Union, and her merchants openly professed the belief that they were to become the metropolis of America without exertion.

Rapid transit only amused them, while raw crops and milled breadstuffs still sought the cheapest rates of freight. They looked at the tabulated figures; they were still shipping their share of the Valley's vastly increased field products. It was not true, they said, with sudden resentment, that they "sold the skin for a groat and bought the tail for a shilling." But they did not look far enough. Improved transportation, denser settlement, labor-saving machinery, had immensely increased the West's producing power. New Orleans should have received and exported an even greater proportion—not merely quantity—of those products of the field. Partly not heeding, and partly unable to help it, she abandoned this magnificent surplus to the growing cities of the West and East. Still more did she fail to notice that the manufactures of the Mississippi and Ohio States had risen from fifty to one hundred and sixty-four millions. She began to observe these facts only as another decade was closing with 1850, when her small import trade had shrunken to less than a third that of Boston and a tenth that of New York.

Her people then began to call out in alarm. Now admitting, now denying, they marked, with a loser's impatience, the progress of other cities at what seemed to be their expense. Boston had surpassed them in numbers; Brooklyn was four-fifths their size; St. Louis, seven-

Old Passage de la Bourse.   Looking toward the French Quarter.

eighths; Cincinnati was but a twenty-fifth behind; Louisville, Chicago, Buffalo, Pittsburg, were coming on with populations of from forty to fifty thousand.   Where were

the days when New Orleans was the commercial empress
of her great valley and heir-apparent to the sovereignty
of the world's trade? New York, Philadelphia, Baltimore,
Liverpool—could they ever be overtaken? American
merchant and Creole property-holder cried to each other
to throw off their lethargy and place New Orleans where
Nature had destined her to sit.

The air was full of diagnoses: There had been too ex-
clusive an attention to the moving of crops; there had
been too much false pride against mercantile pursuits;
sanitation had been neglected; there had not been even
the pretense of a quarantine since 1825; public improvements had been few and trivial; a social exclusiveness
made the town unhomelike and repellant to the higher
order of immigrant; the port charges were suicidal. One
pen even brought out the underlying fact of slave labor,
and contrasted its voiceless acceptation of antiquated
methods of work with the reflecting, outspeaking, acting
liberty of the Northern workman which filled the Northern communities with practical thinkers. The absurd
municipality system of city government, which split the
city into four towns, was rightly blamed for much non-
progression.

Much, too, was the more unjust blame laid at the door
of financiers and capitalists. Railways? But who could
swing a railway from New Orleans, in any direction, that it
would not be better to stretch from some point near the centre of Western supply to some other centre in the manu-

facturing and consuming East ?   Slave labor had handed
over the rich prize of European and New England immigration to the unmonopolized West, and the purely for-
tune-hunting canal-boat and locomotive pushed aside the
slave and his owner and followed the free immigrant.
And, in truth, it was years later, when the outstretched
iron arms of Northern enterprise began to grasp the products of the Southwest itself, that New Orleans capitalists,
with more misgiving than enthusiasm, thrust out their first
railway worthy of the name through the great plantation
State of Mississippi.

Some lamented a lack of banking capital.   But bankers
knew that New York's was comparatively smaller.   Some
cried against summer absenteeism ; but absenteeism was
equally bad in the cities that had thriven most.   Some
pointed to the large proportion of foreigners; but the first
census that gave this proportion showed it but forty-four
and a half per cent. of the whites in New Orleans, against
forty-two in Cincinnati, forty-eight in New York, and
fifty-two in St. Louis.   The truth lay deeper hid.   In
those cities American thought prevailed, and the incoming
foreigner accepted it.   In New Orleans American thought
was foreign, unwelcome, disparaged by the unaspiring,
satirical Creole, and often apologized for by the American,
who found himself a minority in a combination of social
forces oftener in sympathy with European ideas than with
the moral energies and the enthusiastic and venturesome
enterprise of the New World.   Moreover, twenty-eight

thousand slaves and free blacks hampered the spirit of progress by sheer dead weight.

Was it true that the import trade needed only to be cul-

Behind the Old French Market.

tivated? Who should support it beside the planter? And the planter, all powerful as he was, was numerically a small minority, and his favorite investments were land and negroes. The wants of his slaves were only the most

primitive, and their stupid and slovenly eye-service made
the introduction of labor-saving machinery a farce. Who
or what should make an import trade? Not the Southern
valley. Not the West, either; for her imports, she must
have straight lines and prompt deliveries.

Could manufactures be developed? Not easily, at least.
The same fatal shadow fell upon them. The unintelligent,
uneconomical black slave was unavailable for its service;
and to graft upon the slave-burdened South the high-
spirited operatives of other countries was impossible.

What did all this sum up? Stripped of disguises, it
stood a triumph of machinery over slavery that could not
be retrieved, save possibly through a social revolution so
great and apparently so ruinous that the mention of it
kindled a white heat of public exasperation.

All this was emphasized by the Creole. He retained
much power still, as well by his natural force as by his
ownership of real estate and his easy coalition with foreigners of like ideas. He cared little to understand. It
was his pride not to be understood. He divided and paralyzed public sentiment when he could no longer rule it,
and often met the most imperative calls for innovation
with the most unbending conservatism. For every movement was change, and every change carried him nearer
and nearer toward the current of American ideas and to
absorption into their flood, which bore too much the sem-
blance of annihilation. Hold back as he might, the trans-
formation was appallingly swift. And now a new influ-

ence had set in, which above all others was destined to promote, ever more and more, the unity of all the diverse elements of New Orleans society, and their equipment for the task of placing their town in a leading rank among the greatest cities of the world.

XXXIII.

THE SCHOOL-MASTER.

THE year 1841 dates the rise in New Orleans of the modern system of free public schools. It really began in the German-American suburb, Lafayette; but the next year a single school was opened in the Second Municipality " with some dozen scholars of both sexes."

All the way back to the Cession, efforts, more or less feeble, had been made for public education; but all of them lacked that idea of popular and universal benefit which has made the American public school a welcome boon throughout America, not excepting Louisiana. In 1804, an act had passed " to establish a university in the territory of Orleans." The university was to comprise the " college of New Orleans." But seven years later nothing had been done. In 1812, however, there rose on the old Bayou road, a hundred yards or so beyond the former line of the town's rear ramparts, at the corner of St. Claude Street, such a modest Orleans college as $15,000 would build and equip. But it was not free, except to fifty charity scholars. The idea was still that of condescending benevolence, not of a paying investment by society for its own protection and elevation. Ten years later this was the only school in the city of a public character. In 1826, there were three small schools where "all the branches of a polite education" were taught. Two of these were in the old Ursuline convent. A fourth finds mention in 1838, but the college seems to have disappeared.

Still the mass of educable youth,—the children who played "oats, peas, beans," with French and German and Irish accents, about the countless sidewalk doorsteps of a city of one and two-story cottages (it was almost such); the girls who carried their little brothers and sisters on one elbow and hip and stared in at weddings and funerals; the boys whose kite-flying and games were full of terms and outcries in mongrel French, and who abandoned everything at the wild clangor of bells and ran to fires where the volunteer firemen dropped the hose and wounded and killed each other in pitched battles; the ill-kept lads who risked their lives daily five months of the year swimming in the yellow whirlpools of the Mississippi among the wharves and flat-boats, who, naked and dripping, dodged the dignified police that stalked them among the cotton bales, who robbed mocking-birds' nests and orange and fig-trees, and trapped nonpareils and cardinals, orchard-orioles and indigo-birds in the gardens of Lafayette and the sub-urban fields,—these had not been reached, had not been sought by the educator. The public recognition of a common vital interest in a common elevation was totally lacking.

17

At length this feeling was aroused.   Men of public spirit spoke and acted ; and such pioneers as Peters, Burke, Touro, Martin, De Bow, and the Creoles Dimitry, Forstall, Gayarre, and others are gratefully remembered by a later generation for their labors in the cause of education.   In the beginning of 1842 there were in the American quarter 300 children in private schools and 2,000 in none.   At its close, the public schools of this quarter and Lafayette had over 1,000 pupils.   In the next year, there were over 1,300 ; in 1844, there were 1,800.   In 1845, the University of Louisiana was really established.   The medical department had already an existence ; this branch and that of law were in full operation in 1847, and Creole and American sat side by side before their lecturers.

Meanwhile the impulse for popular enlightenment took another good direction.   In 1842, Mr. B. F. French threw open a library to the public, which in four years numbered 7,500 volumes.   The State Library was formed, with 3,000 volumes, for the use, mainly, of the Legislature.   The City Library, also 3,000 volumes, was formed.   In 1848 it numbered 7,500 volumes ; but it was intended principally for the schools, and was not entirely free.   An association threw open a collection of 2,000 volumes.   An historical society was revived.   In 1846 and 1847 public lectures were given and heartily supported ; but, in 1848, a third series was cut short by a terrible epidemic of cholera.   About the same time, the " Fisk " Library of 6,000 volumes, with " a building for their reception," was offered to the city. But enthusiasm had declined. The gift was neglected, and as late as 1854, the city was still without a single entirely free library.

In 1850 there was but one school, Sunday-school, or public library in Louisiana to each 73,966 persons, or 100 volumes to each 2,310 persons. In Rhode Island, there were eleven and a half times as many books to each person. In Massachusetts, there were 100 volumes to every 188 persons. In the pioneer State of Michigan, without any large city, there was a volume to every fourth person. True, in Louisiana there were 100 volumes to every 1,218 *free* persons, but this only throws us back upon the fact that 245,000 persons were totally without books and were forbidden by law to read.

It is pleasanter to know that the city's public schools grew rapidly in numbers and efficiency, and that, even when her library facilities were so meagre, the proportion of youth in these schools was larger than in Baltimore or Cincinnati, only slightly inferior to St. Louis and New York, and decidedly surpassed only in Philadelphia and Boston. In the old French quarter, the approach of school-hour saw thousands of Creole children, satchel in hand, on their way to some old live-oak-shaded colonial villa, or to some old theatre once the scene of nightly gambling and sword-cane fights, or to some ancient ball-room where the now faded quadroons had once shone in splendor and waltzed with the mercantile and official dignitaries of city and State, or to some bright, new school building, all windows

and verandas. Thither they went for an English education. It was not first choice, but it was free, and—the
father and mother admitted, with an amiable shrug—it
was also best.

The old, fierce enmity against the English tongue and
American manners began to lose its practical weight and
to be largely a matter of fireside sentiment. The rich
Creole, both of plantation and town, still drew his inspira-
tions from French tradition,—not from books,—and sought
both culture and pastime in Paris. His polish heightened;
his language improved; he dropped the West Indian softness that had crept into his pronunciation, and the African-
isms of his black nurse. His children still babbled them,
but they were expected to cast them off about the time of
their first communion. However, the suburban lands were
sold, old town and down-town property was sinking in
value, the trade with Latin countries languished, and the
rich Creole was only one here and there among throngs of
humbler brethren who were learning the hard lessons of
pinched living. To these an English-American training
was too valuable to be refused. They took kindly to the
American's counting-room desk. They even began to
emigrate across Canal Street.

XXXIV.

NOT schools only, but churches, multiplied rapidly. There was a great improvement in public order. Affrays were still common ; the Know-Nothing movement came on, and a few "thugs" terrorized the city with campaign broils, beating, stabbing, and shooting. Base political leaders and spoilsmen utilized these disorders, and they reached an unexpected climax and end one morning confronted by a vigilance committee, which had, under cover of night, seized the town arsenal behind the old Cabildo and barricaded the approaches to the Place d'Armes with uptorn paving-stones. But riots were no longer a feature of the city. It was no longer required that all the night-watch within a mile's circuit should rally at the sound of a rattle. Fire-engines were no longer needed to wet down huge mobs that threatened to demolish the Carondelet Street brokers' shops or the Cuban cigar stores. Drunken bargemen had ceased to swarm by many hundreds against the peace and dignity of the State, and the publicity and respectability of many other vicious practices disappeared.

Communication with the outside world was made much

easier, prompter, and more frequent by the growth of railroads.   Both the average Creole and the average American became more refined.   The two types lost some of their points of difference.   The American ceased to crave entrance into Creole society, having now separate circles of his own ; and when they mingled it was on more equal terms, and the Creole was sometimes the proselyte. They were one on the great question that had made the American southerner the exasperated champion of ideas contrary to the ground principles of American social order. The New Orleans American was apt, moreover, by this time to be New-Orleans born.   He had learned some of the Creole's lethargy, much of his love of pleasure and his child-ish delight in pageantry.   St. Charles Street—the centre of the American-quarter, the focus of American theatres and American indulgences in decanter and dice — seemed strangely un-American when Mardigras filled it with dense crowds, tinsel, rouge, grotesque rags, Circean masks, fool's-caps and harlequin colors, lewdness, mock music, and tipsy buffoonery.   " We want," said one American of strange ambition, " to make our city the Naples of America."

By and by a cloud darkened the sky.   Civil war came on.   The Creole, in that struggle, was little different from the Southerner at large.   A little more impetuous, it may be, a little more gayly reckless, a little more prone to rea-son from desire ; gallant, brave, enduring, faithful ; son, grandson, great-grandson, of good soldiers, and a better soldier every way and truer to himself than his courageous

forefathers.   He was early at Pensacola.   He was at
Charleston when the first gun was fired.   The first hero
that came back from the Virginia Peninsula on his shield
was a Creole.   It was often he who broke the quiet
along the Potomac, now with song and now with rifle-shot.
He was at Bull-Run, at Shiloh, on all those blood-steeped
fields around Richmond.   He marched and fought with
Stonewall Jackson.   At Mobile, at the end, he was there.
No others were quite so good for siege guns and water-
batteries.   What fields are not on his folded banners?
He went through it all.   But we will not follow him.
Neither will we write the history of his town in those
dread days.   Arming, marching, blockade, siege, surrender,
military occupation, grass-grown streets, hungry women,
darkened homes, broken hearts,—let us not write the
chapter ; at least, not yet.

The war passed.   The bitter days of Reconstruction followed.   They, too, must rest unrecounted.   The sky is
brightening again.   The love of the American Union has
come back to the Creole and the American of New Orleans
stronger, for its absence, than it ever was before ; stronger,
founded in a triple sense of right, necessity, and choice.

The great south gate of the Mississippi stood, in 1880,
a city of two hundred and sixteen thousand people, and
has been growing ever since.   Only here and there a broad
avenue, with double roadway and slender grassy groves of
forest trees between, marks the old dividing lines of the
faubourgs that have from time to time been gathered

within her boundaries. Her streets measure five hundred and sixty-six miles of length. One hundred and forty miles of street railway traverse them. Her wealth in 1882, was $112,000,000. Her imports are light, but no other American city save New York has such an annual export. Her harbor, varying from 60 to 280 feet in depth, and from 1,500 to 3,000 feet in width, measures twelve miles in length on either shore, and more than half of this is in actual use. In 1883, over 2,000,000 bales of cotton passed through her gates, to home or foreign markets.

One of the many developments in the world's commerce, unforeseen by New Orleans in her days of over-confidence, was the increase in the size of sea-going vessels. It had been steady and rapid, but was only noticed when the larger vessels began to shun the bars and mud-lumps of the river's mouths. In 1852 there were, for weeks, nearly forty ships aground there, suffering detentions of from two days to eight weeks. It is true, some slack-handed attention had been given to these bars from the earliest times. Even in 1721, M. de Pauger, a French engineer, had recommended a system for scouring them away, by confining the current, not materially different from that which proved so successful one hundred and fifty years later. The United States Government made surveys and reports in 1829, '37, '39, '47, and '51. But, while nature was now shoaling one "pass" and now deepening another, the effort to keep them open artificially was not efficiently or persistently made. Dredging, harrowing, jettying, and

side-canalling—all were proposed, and some were tried ;
but nothing of a permanent character was effected. In
1853 vessels were again grounding on the bars, where
some of them remained for months.

At length, in 1874, Mr. James B. Eads came forward
with a proposition to secure a permanent channel in one
of the passes, twenty-eight feet deep, by a system of jet-
ties.   He met with strenuous opposition from professional
and unprofessional sources, but overcame both man and
nature, and in July, 1879, successfully completed the work
which has made him world-famous and which promises to
New Orleans once more a magnificent future.   Through
a " pass " where a few years ago vessels of ten feet draft
went aground, a depth of thirty feet is assured, and there
are no ships built that may not come to her wharves.
Capital has responded to this great change.   Railroads
have hurried and are hurrying down upon the city, and
have joined her with Mexico and California ; manufactur-
ing interests are multiplying steadily ; new energies, new
ambitions, are felt by her people ; for the first time within
a quarter of a century buildings in the heart of the town
are being torn down to make room for better.   As these
lines are being written the city is engrossed in preparations for a universal exposition projected on the largest
scale ; the very Creole himself is going to ask the world to
come and see him.   In every department of life and every
branch of society there is earnest, intelligent effort to remove
old drawbacks and prepare for the harvests of richer years.

XXXV.

THE people of New Orleans take pride in Canal Street. It is to the modern town what the Place d'Armes was to the old. Here stretch out in long parade, in variety of height and color, the great retail stores, displaying their silken and fine linen and golden seductions; and the fair Creole and American girls, and the self-depreciating American mothers, and the majestic Creole matrons, all black lace and alabaster, swarm and hum and push in and out and flit here and there among the rich things, and fine things, the novelties and the bargains. Its eighteen-feet sidewalks are loftily roofed from edge to edge by continuous balconies that on gala-days are stayed up with extra scantlings, and yet seem ready to come splintering down under the crowd of parasolled ladies sloping upward on them from front to back in the fashion of the amphitheatre. Its two distinct granite-paved roadways are each forty feet wide, and the tree-bordered "neutral ground" between measures fifty-four feet across. It was "neutral" when it divided between the French quarter and the

American at the time when their "municipality" governments were distinct from each other.

In Canal Street, well-nigh all the street-car lines in town begin and end. The Grand Opera House is here; also, the Art Union. The club-houses glitter here. If Jackson Square has one bronze statue, Canal Street has another, and it is still an open question which is the worst. At the base of Henry Clay's pedestal, the people rally to hear the demagogues in days of political fever, and the tooth-paste orator in nights of financial hypertrophy. Here are the grand reviews. Here the resplendent Mystic Krewe marches by calcium lights on carnival nights up one roadway and down the other, and

> "Perfume and flowers fall in showers,
> That lightly rain from ladies' hands."

Here is the huge granite custom-house, that "never is but always to be" finished. Here is a row of stores monumental to the sweet memory of the benevolent old Portuguese Jew whom Newport, Rhode Island, as well as New Orleans, gratefully honors—Judah Touro. Here sit the flower *marchandes*, making bouquets of jasmines and roses, clove-pinks, violets, and lady-slippers. Here the Creole boys drink mead, and on the balconies above maidens and their valentines sip sherbets in the starlight. Here only, in New Orleans, the American "bar" puts on a partial disguise. Here is the way to West End and to Spanish Fort, little lakeside spots of a diminished Coney Island

sort. Here the gay carriage-parties turn northwestward,
scurrying away to the races. Yea, here the funeral train
breaks into a trot toward the cemeteries of Metairie Ridge.
Here is Christ's Church, with its canopied weddings.
Here the ring-politician mounts perpetual guard. Here
the gambler seeks whom he may induce to walk around into
his parlor in the Rue Royale or St. Charles Street. And
here, in short, throng the members of the great New Orleans
Creole-American house of " Walker, Doolittle & Co."

One does not need to be the the oldest resident to remember when this neutral ground in Canal Street was still
a place of tethered horses, roaming goats, and fluttering
lines of drying shirts and petticoats. In those days an
old mule used to drag his dejected way slowly round and
round in an unchanging circle on the shabby grassed avenue, just behind the spot where the statue of Henry Clay
was later erected by good Whigs in 1856. An aged and
tattered negro was the mule's ringmaster, and an artesian
well was the object of his peaceful revolution.

No effort deeply to probe the city's site had ever before
been made, nor has there been any later attempt thus to
draw up the pre-historic records of the Delta. The alluvial surface deposit is generally two or three feet thick,
and rests on a substratum of uniform and tenacious blue
clay. The well in Canal Street found this clay fifteen feet
deep. Below it lay four feet more of the same clay mixed
with woody matter. Under this was a mixture of sand
and clay ten feet thick, resembling the annual deposits of

the river. Beneath this was found, one after another, continual, irregular alternations of these clay strata, sometimes a foot, sometimes sixty feet thick, and layers of sand and shells and of mixtures of these with clay. Sometimes a stratum of quicksand was passed. At five hundred and eighty-two feet was encountered a layer of hard pan; but throughout no masses of rock were found, only a few water-worn pebbles and some contorted and perforated stones. No abundance of water flowed. Still, in the shabby, goat-haunted neutral ground above, gaped at by the neutral crowd, in the wide, blinding heat of midsummer, the long lever continued to creak round its tremulous circle. At length it stopped. At a depth of six hundred and thirty feet the well was abandoned—for vague reasons left to the custody of tradition; some say the mule died, some say the negro.

However, the work done was not without value. It must have emphasized the sanitary necessity for an elaborate artificial drainage of the city's site, and it served to contradict a very prevalent and solicitous outside belief that New Orleans was built on a thin crust of mud, which she might at any moment break through, when towers, spires, and all would ingloriously disappear. The continual alternations of tough clay and loose sand and shells in such variable thicknesses gave a clear illustration of the conditions of Delta soil that favor the undermining of the Mississippi banks and their fall into the river at low stages of water, levees being often carried with them.

These cavings are not generally *crevasses*. A crevasse
is commonly the result of the levee yielding to the pressure of the river's waters, heaped up against it often to the
height of ten or fifteen feet above the level of the land.
But the caving-in of old levees requires their replacement
by new and higher ones on the lower land farther back,

A Crevasse. (Story's Plantation, 1882.)

and a crevasse often occurs through the weakness of a
new levee which is not yet solidified, or whose covering
of tough Bermuda turf has not yet grown. The fact is
widely familiar, too, that when a craw-fish has burrowed
in a levee, the water of the river may squirt in and out of
this little tunnel, till a section of the levee becomes satu-
rated and softened, and sometimes slides shoreward bodily

from its base, and lets in the flood,—roaring, leaping, and tumbling over the rich plantations and down into the swamp behind them, levelling, tearing up, drowning, destroying, and sweeping away as it goes.

New Orleans may be inundated either by a crevasse or by the rise of backwater on its northern side from Lake Pontchartrain. Bayou St. John is but a prehistoric crevasse minus only the artificial levee. A long-prevailing southeast wind will obstruct the outflow of the lake's waters through the narrow passes by which they commonly reach the Gulf of Mexico, and the rivers and old crevasses emptying into the lake from the north and east will be virtually poured into the streets of New Orleans. A violent storm blowing across Pontchartrain from the north produces the same result. At certain seasons, the shores of river, lake, and canals have to be patrolled day and night to guard the wide, shallow basin in which the city lies from the insidious encroachments of the waters that overhang it on every side.

It is difficult, in a faithful description, to avoid giving an exaggerated idea of these floods. Certainly, large portions of the city are inundated ; miles of streets become canals. The waters rise into yards and gardens and then into rooms. Skiffs enter the poor man's parlor and bedroom to bring the morning's milk or to carry away to higher ground his goods and chattels. All manner of loose stuff floats about the streets ; the house-cat sits on the gate-post ; huge rats come swimming, in mute and loathsome despair, from that house to this one, and are pelted to death from the windows. Even snakes seek the same asylum. Those who have the choice avoid such districts, and the city has consequently lengthened out awkwardly along the higher grounds down, and especially up, the river shore.

But the town is not ingulfed; life is not endangered; trade goes on in its main districts mostly dry-shod, and the merchant goes and comes between his home and his counting-room as usual in the tinkling street-cars, merely catching glimpses of the water down the cross streets.

The humbler classes, on the other hand, suffer severely. Their gardens and poultry are destroyed, their houses and household goods are damaged; their working days are discounted. The rich and the authorities, having defaulted in the ounce of preventive, come forward with their ineffectual pound of cure; relief committees are formed and skiffs ply back and forth distributing bread to the thus doubly humbled and doubly damaged poor.

No considerable increase of sickness seems to follow these overflows. They cannot more completely drench so ill-drained a soil than would any long term of rainy weather; but it hardly need be said that neither condition is healthful under a southern sky.

In the beginning of the town's existence, the floods came almost yearly, and for a long time afterward they were frequent. The old moat and palisaded embankment around the Spanish town did not always keep them out.

There was a disastrous one in 1780, when the Creoles were strained to the utmost to bear the burdens of their daring young Governor Galvez's campaigns against the British. Another occurred in 1785, when Miró was governor; another in 1791, the last year of his incumbency; another in 1799. All these came from river crevasses above the town. The last occurred near where Carrollton, now part of New Orleans, was afterward built. Another overflow, in 1813, came from a crevasse only a mile or two above this one.

Next followed the noted overflow of May, 1816. The same levee that had broken in 1799 was undermined by the current, which still strikes the bank at Carrollton with immense power; it gave way and the floods of the Mississippi poured through the break. On the fourth day afterward, the waters had made their way across sugar-fields and through swamps and into the rear of the little city, had covered the suburbs of Gravier, Trémé, and St. Jean with from three to five feet of their turbid, yellow flood, and were crawling up toward the front of the river-side suburbs—Montegut, La Course, Ste. Marie, and Marigny. In those days, the corner of Canal and Chartres Streets was only some three hundred yards from the river shore. The flood came up to it. One could take a skiff at that point and row to Dauphine Street, down Dauphine to Bienville, down Bienville to Burgundy, in Burgundy to St. Louis Street, from St. Louis to Rampart, and so throughout the rear suburbs, now the Quadroon quarter.

18

The breach was stopped by sinking in it a three-masted vessel. The waters found vent through Bayous St. John and Bienvenu to the lake; but it was twenty-five days before they were quite gone. This twelvemonth was the healthiest in a period of forty years.

In the Quadroon Quarter.

In 1831, a storm blew the waters of Lake Pontchartrain up to within six hundred yards of the levee. The same thing occurred in October, 1837, when bankruptcy as well as back waters swamped the town. The same waters were driven almost as far in 1844, and again in 1846.

It would seem as if town pride alone would have seized a spade and thrown up a serviceable levee around the city.

But town pride in New Orleans was only born about 1836, and was a puny child. Not one American in five looked on the place as his permanent home. As for those who did, the life they had received from their fathers had become modified. Some of them were a native generation. Creole contact had been felt. The same influences, too, of climate, landscape, and institutions, that had made the Creole unique was de-Saxonizing the American of the "Second Municipality," and giving special force to those two traits which everywhere characterized the slave-holder —improvidence, and that feudal self-completeness which looked with indolent contempt upon public co-operative measures.

The Creole's answer to suggestive inquiry concerning the prevention of overflows, it may easily be guessed, was a short, warm question: "How?" He thought one ought to tell him. He has ten good "cannots" to one small "can"—or once had; the proportion is better now, and so is the drainage; and still, heat, moisture, malaria, and provincial exile make a Creole of whoever settles down beside him.

In 1836, a municipal draining company was formed, and one draining wheel erected at Bayou St. John. In 1838, a natural drain behind the American quarter was broadened and deepened into a foul ditch known as Melpomene Canal. And in 1849, came the worst inundation the city has ever suffered.

XXXVI.

SAUVÉ'S CREVASSE.

ON the 3d of May, 1849, the Mississippi was higher than it had been before in twenty-one years. Every here and there it was licking the levee's crown, swinging heavily around the upper end of its great bends, gliding in wide, enormous volume down upon the opposite bank below, heaving its vast weight and force against the earthen barrier, fretting, quaking, recoiling, boiling like a pot, and turning again and billowing away like a monstrous yellow serpent, crested with its long black line of driftwood, to throw itself once more against the farther bank, in its mad, blind search for outlet.

Everywhere, in such times, the anxious Creole planter may be seen, broad-hatted and swarthy, standing on his levee's top. All night the uneasy lantern of the patrol flits along the same line. Rills of seepage water wet the road—which in Louisiana always runs along against the levee's inner side—and here and there make miry places. "Cribs" are being built around weak spots. Sand-bags are held in readiness. The huge, ungainly cane-carts, with their high, broad-tired wheels and flaring blue bodies,

A Full River. (Lower front corner of the Old Town.)

each drawn by three sunburned mules abreast, come lumbering from the sugar-house yard with loads of *bagasse*, with which to give a fibrous hold to the hasty earthworks called for by the hour's emergency. Here, at the most dangerous spot, the muscular strength of the estate is grouped ; a saddled horse stands hitched to the road-side fence ; the overseer is giving his short, emphatic orders in the negro French of the plantations, and the black man, glancing ever and anon upon him with his large brown eye, comes here and goes there, *li vini 'ci, li courri là*. Will they be able to make the levee stand ? Nobody knows.

In 1849, some seventeen miles above New Orleans by the river's course, and on the same side of the stream, was Sauvé's plantation. From some cause, known or unknown, —sometimes the fact is not even suspected,—the levee along its river-front was weak. In the afternoon of the 3d of May, the great river suddenly burst through it, and, instantly defying all restraints, plunged down over the land, roaring, rolling, writhing, sprawling, whirling, over pastures and cane-fields and rice-fields, through groves and negro quarters and sugar-houses, slipping through rose-hedged lanes and miles of fence, gliding through willow jungles and cypress forests, on and on, to smite in rear and flank the city that, seventeen miles away, lay peering alertly over its front breastworks. The people of the town were not, at first, concerned. They believed and assured each other the water would find its way across into

Lake Pontchartrain without coming down upon them. The Americans exceeded the Creoles in absolute torpor. They threw up no line behind their municipality. Every day that passed saw the swamp filling more and more with yellow water; presently it crawled up into the suburbs, and when the twelfth day had gone by, Rampart Street, the old town's rear boundary, was covered.

The Creoles, in their quarter, had strengthened the small levee of canal Carondelet on its lower side and shut off the advancing flood from the district beyond it; but Lafayette and the older American quarter were completely exposed. The water crept on daily for a fortnight longer. In the suburb Bouligny, afterward part of Jefferson or the Sixth District, it reached to Camp Street. In Lafayette, it stopped within thirty yards of where these words are being written, and withdrawing toward the forest, ran along behind Bacchus (Baronne) Street, sometimes touching Carondelet, till it reached Canal Street, crossed that street between Royal and Bourbon, and thence stretched downward and backward to the Old Basin. "About two hundred and twenty inhabited squares were flooded, more than two thousand tenements surrounded by water, and a population of nearly twelve thousand souls driven from their homes or compelled to live an aquatic life of much privation and suffering."

In the meantime, hundreds of men, white and black, were constantly at the breach in the levee, trying to close it. Pickets, sand-bags, *bagasse*, were all in vain. Seven hundred feet of piling were driven, but unskilfully placed; a ship's hull was filled with stone and sunk in the half-closed opening, but the torrent burrowed around it and swept away the works. Other unskilled efforts failed, and only on the third of June was professional scientific aid called in, and seventeen days afterward the crevasse was closed.

At length, the long-submerged streets and sidewalks rose slimily out of the retreating waters, heavy rains fell opportunely and washed into the swamp the offensive deposits that had threatened a second distress, and the people set about repairing their disasters. The streets were in sad dilapidation. The Second Municipality alone levied, in the following year, four hundred thousand dollars to cover "actual expenditures on streets, wharves, and crevasses." The wharves were, most likely, in the main, new work. A levee was thrown up behind the municipality along the line of Claiborne Street and up Felicity road to Carondelet Street.

Still overflows came, and came, and overcame. A serious one occurred only four years ago.[1] At such times, the fortunate are nobly generous to the unfortunate; but the distress passes, the emotional impulses pass with it, and precautions for the future are omitted or soon fall into neglect. The inundation of 1880 simply overran the dilapidated top of a neglected levee on the town's lake

_____

[1] 1880.

side. The uneconomical habits of the old South still cling.
Private burdens are but faintly recognized, and the next
norther may swamp the little fortunes of the city's hard-
working poor.

The hopeful in New Orleans look for an early day when
a proper drainage system shall change all this,—a system
which shall include underground sewerage and complete
the levee, already partly made, which is to repeat on a
greatly enlarged scale, above and below the city and along
the lake shore behind it, the old wall and moat that once
surrounded the Spanish town in Canal, Rampart, and Esplanade Streets. The present system consists merely of a
poor and partial surface drainage in open street-gutters,
emptying into canals at whose further end the waters are
lifted over the rear levees by an appliance of old Dutch
paddle-wheel pumps run by steam. Even the sudden
heavy showers that come with their singeing lightnings
and ear-cracking peals of thunder, are enough, at present,
to overflow the streets of the whole town, often from sill
to sill of opposite houses and stores, holding the life of a
great city water-bound for hours, making strange arch-
way and door-way groups of beggar and lady, clerk, fop,
merchant, artisan, fruit-peddler, negro porter, priest,
tattered girl, and every other sort of fine or pitiful human
nature.

An adequate system, comprising a thorough under-
drainage, would virtually raise the city's whole plain ten
feet, and give a character of soil under foot incalculably

valuable for the improvement it would effect in the health and energies of the people. Such a system is entirely feasible, is within the people's means, has been tested elsewhere, extensively and officially approved, and requires only the subscription of capital.

But we go astray. We have got out upon the hither side of those volcanoes of civil war and reconstruction which it were wiser for a time yet to stop short of. Let us draw back once more for a last view of the "Crescent City's" earlier and calmer, though once tumultuous and all too tragic, past.

XXXVII.

THE DAYS OF PESTILENCE.

THE New Orleans resident congratulates himself—and
he does well—that he is not as other men are, in
other great cities, as to breathing-room. The desperate
fondness with which the Creole still clings to domestic
isolation has passed into the sentiment of all types of the
city's life; and as the way is always open for the town,
with just a little river-sand filling, to spread farther and
farther, there is no huddling in New Orleans, or only very
little here and there.

There is assurance of plenty not only as to space, but
also as to time. Time may be money, but money is not
everything, and so there never has been much crowding
over one another's heads about business centres, never any
living in sky-reaching strata. The lassitude which loads
every warm, damp breeze that blows in across the all-sur-
rounding marsh and swamp has always been against what
an old New Orleans writer calls "knee-cracking stair-
ways." Few houses lift their roofs to dizzy heights, and
a third-story bedroom is not near enough to be coveted by
many.

Shortly before the war—and the case is not materially changed in New Orleans to-day—the number of inmates to a dwelling was in the proportion of six and a half to one. In St. Louis, it was seven and three-quarters; in Cincinnati, it was more than eight; in Boston, nearly nine; and in New York, over thirteen and a half. The number of persons to the acre was a little more than forty-five. In Philadelphia, it was eighty; in Boston, it was eighty-two; in New York, it was one hundred and thirty-five.

The climate never would permit such swarming in New Orleans. Neither would the badly scavenged streets or the soil which, just beneath, reeks with all the foul liquids that human and brute life can produce in an unsewered city. It is fortunate that the average New Orleans dwelling is loosely thrown together, built against sun and rain, not wind and frost. This, with the ample spacings between houses, and an open plain all round, insures circulation of air—an air that never blows extremes of hot or cold.

It is true the minimum temperature is lower than that on the sea-coast of California, in part of Arizona, and in South Florida. That of the Gulf coasts and the Atlantic shores of Georgia and South Carolina is the same. But in every other part of the United States it is lower. Once only the thermometer has been known to sink to sixteen degrees Fahrenheit. Its mean January temperature is fifty-five degrees to sixty degrees Fahrenheit, milder than that of any other notable city in the Union, except

Galveston and Mobile, which have the same. Only Middle
and Southern Florida have a warmer midwinter. As to
its summers, every State and Territory, except the five
New England States east and north of Connecticut, expe-
riences in some portion of it a higher maximum temperature than the land of the Creoles, and the entire country
as high a temperature, except parts of California, Oregon,
Washington Territory, and two or three regions directly
within the Rocky Mountains. Even its mean temperature
in the hottest month of the year, July, is only the same,
eighty to eighty-five degrees, as that in every part of the
South that is not mountainous, even to the mouth of the
Ohio, with the Indian Territory and two-thirds of Kansas.
Only three times since 1819 has it risen to one hundred
degrees, and never beyond. Whatever wind prevails
comes tempered by the waters and wet lands over which
it has blown. The duration of this moderate heat, however, is what counts. The mean temperature of New
Orleans for the year exceeds that of any region not on the
Gulf. It is exceeded only in southernmost Florida. That
of Arkansas, middle Mississippi, middle Georgia, and South
Carolina is ten degrees cooler, and the northeastern quarter of Alabama, North Georgia, and Western North Carolina have a mean fifteen, twenty, and in the mountainous
parts, thirty and more degrees lower. The humidity,
moreover, is against strong vitality. The country is not
to be called a rainy one ; there is no rainy season ; but the
rains, when they come, are very heavy. Over five feet depth

of water falls yearly on this land of swamps and marshes south of the thirty-first parallel between Lake Sabine and Apalachee Bay; a fall from four to six times as great as the rainfall in the arid regions of the far West, more than twice the average for the whole area of the United States, and greater than that experienced by over ninety-eight per cent. of the whole population. The air's diminished evaporating powers make it less cooling to man and beast in summer and more chilling in winter than drier winds at greater and lower temperatures would be, and it comes always more or less charged with that uncanny quality which Creoles, like all other North Americans, maintain to be never at home, but always next door—malaria.

The city does not tremble with ague; but malarial fevers stand high in the annual tables of mortality, almost all complaints are complicated by more or less malarial influence, and the reduction of vital force in the daily life of the whole population is such as few residents, except physicians, appreciate. Lately, however,—we linger in the present but a moment,—attention has turned to the fact that the old Creole life, on ground floors, in a damp, warm climate, over an undrained clay soil, has given more victims to malarial and tubercular diseases than yellow fever has claimed, and efforts to remove these conditions or offset their ill effects are giving a yearly improving public health.

What figures it would require truthfully to indicate the

early insalubrity of New Orleans it would be hard to
guess. Governor Perier, in 1726, and the Baron Carondelet, toward the close of the last century, stand alone as
advocates for measures to reduce malarial and putrid fevers. As time wore on, partial surface drainage, some
paving, some improvement in house-building, wiser domestic life, the gradual retreat of the dank forest and
undergrowth, a better circulation of air, and some reduction of humidity, had their good effects. Drainage canals
—narrow, shallow, foul, ill-placed things—began to be
added one by one. When a system of municipal cleansing came in, it was made as vicious as ingenuity could
contrive it; or, let us say, as bad as in other American
cities of the time.

Neither the Creole nor the American ever accepts sep-
ulture in the ground of Orleans Parish. Only the He-
brew, whose religious law will not take no for an answer,
and the pauper, lie down in its undrained soil. The
tombs stand above ground. They are now made of brick
or stone only ; but in earlier days wood entered into their
construction, and they often fell into decay so early as to
expose the bones of the dead. Every day the ground,
which the dead shunned, became more and more poisonous, and the city spread out its homes of the living more
and more over the poisoned ground. In 1830, the population of New Orleans was something over forty-six thousand ; her life was busy, her commerce great, her precautions against nature's penalties for human herding about

equal to nothing. She was fully ripe for the visitation that was in store.

In that year the Asiatic cholera passed around the shores of the Caspian Sea, entered European Russia, and moved slowly westward, preceded by terror and followed by lamentation. In October, 1831, it was in England. In January, 1832, it swept through London. It passed into Scotland, into Ireland, France, Spain, Italy. It crossed the Atlantic and ravaged the cities of its western shore; and, on the 25th of October, it reached New Orleans.

An epidemic of yellow fever had been raging, and had not yet disappeared. Many of the people had fled from it. The population was reduced to about thirty-five thousand. How many victims the new pestilence carried off can never be known; but six thousand, over one-sixth of the people, fell in twenty days. On some days five hundred persons died. For once, the rallying-ground of the people was not the Place d'Armes. The cemeteries were too small. Trenches took the place of graves; the dead were hauled to them, uncoffined, in cart-loads and dumped in. Large numbers were carried by night to the river-side, weighted with stones from the ballast-piles abreast the idle shipping, and thrown into the Mississippi. The same mortality in New Orleans with its present population would carry off, in three weeks, thirty-nine thousand victims. The New Basin was being dug by hand. Hundreds of Irish were standing here in water and mud and sun, throwing up the corrupted soil with

19

their shovels, and the havoc among them, says tradition, was awful.

The history of the town shows that years of much summer-digging have always been years of great mortality. In 1811, when Carondelet's old canal was cleaned out, seven per cent. of the people died. In 1818, when it was cleaned out again, seven per cent. again died. In 1822, when its cleaning out was again begun, eight and a half per cent. died. In 1833, when, the year after the great cholera fatality, the New Canal was dug to the lake, eight and a half per cent. again died. In 1837, when many draining trenches were dug, seven per cent. died. In 1847, there was much new ditching, Melpomene Canal was cleaned out, and over eight per cent. of the people died. The same work went on through '48 and '49, and seven and eight per cent. died. But never before or after 1832 did death recruit his pale armies by so frightful a conscription, in this plague-haunted town, as marked that year of double calamity, when, from a total population of but fifty-five thousand, present and absent, over eight thousand fell before their Asian and African destroyers.

XXXVIII.

THREE-QUARTERS of a century had passed over the little Franco-Spanish town, hidden under the Mississippi's downward-retreating bank in the edge of its Delta swamp on Orleans Island, before the sallow spectre of yellow fever was distinctly recognized in her streets and in her darkened chambers.

That it had come and gone earlier, but unidentified, is altogether likely. In 1766 especially, the year in which Ulloa came with his handful of Havanese soldiers to take possession for Spain, there was an epidemic which at least resembled the great West Indian scourge. Under the commercial concessions that followed, the town expanded into a brisk port. Trade with the West Indies grew, and in 1796, the yellow fever was confronted and called by name.

From that date it appeared frequently if not yearly, and between that date and the present day twenty-four lighter and thirteen violent epidemics have marked its visitations. At their own horrid caprice they came and went. In 1821, a quarantine of some sort was established, and it was continued until 1825; but it did not keep out the plague, and it was then abandoned for more than thirty years. Between 1837 and 1843, fifty-five hundred deaths occurred from the fever. In the summer and fall of 1847, over twenty-eight hundred people perished by it. In the second half of 1848, eight hundred and seventy-two were its victims. It had barely disappeared when cholera entered again and carried off forty-one hundred. A month after its disappearance,—in August, 1849,—the fever returned; and when, at the end of November, it had destroyed seven hundred and forty-four persons, the cholera once more appeared; and by the end of 1850 had added eighteen hundred and fifty-one to the long rolls.

In the very midst of these visitations, it was the confident conviction and constant assertion of the average New Orleans citizen, Creole or American, on his levee, in the St. Charles rotunda, at his counting-room desk, in the columns of his newspaper, and in his family circle, that his town was one of the healthiest in the world. The fatality of the epidemics was principally among the unacclimated. He was not insensible to their sufferings, he was famous for his care of the sick; the town was dotted with orphan asylums. But in this far-away corner crucial comparisons escaped him. The Creole did not readily take the fever, and, taking it, commonly recovered. He had, and largely retains still, an absurd belief in his entire immunity from attack. When he has it, it is something else. As for strangers,—he threw up his palms and eyebrows,—nobody asked them to come to New Orleans. The mind of the American turned only to commerce; and the commercial value of a well-authenticated low death-rate he totally overlooked. Every summer might bring plague—granted; but winter brought trade, wealth. It thundered and tumbled through the streets like a surf. The part of a good citizen seemed to be to shut his eyes tightly and drown comment and debate with loud assertions of the town's salubrity.

It was in these days that a certain taste for books showed itself, patronized and dominated by commerce. De Bow's excellent monthly issue, the *Commercial Review of the South and West*, was circulating its invaluable statistics and its pro-Southern deductions in social and political science. Judah P. Benjamin wrote about sugar; so did Valcour-Aime; Riddell treated of Mississippi River deposits, etc.; Maunsell White gave reminiscences of flat-boat navigation; Chief Justice Martin wrote on contract of sale; E. J. Forstall on Louisiana history in French archives; and a great many anonymous "Ladies of New Orleans" and "Gentlemen of New Orleans" and elsewhere, upon the absorbing topic of slavery—to while away the time, as it were. "New Orleans, disguise the fact as we may," wrote De Bow in 1846, "has had abroad the reputation of being a great charnel-house. . . . We meet this libel with facts." But he gave no figures. In January, 1851, the mayor officially pronounced the city " perfectly healthy during the past year," etc., omitting to say that the mortality had been three times as high as a moderate death-rate would have been. A few medical men alone,—Barton, Symonds, Fenner, Axson,—had begun to drag from oblivion the city's vital statistics and to publish facts that should have alarmed any community. But the

A Cemetery Walk.   (Tombs and " Ovens.")

blind are not frightened with ghosts. Barton showed that the mortality of 1849, *over and above* the deaths by cholera, had been about twice the common average of Boston, New York, Philadelphia, or Charleston. What then? Nothing. He urged under-ground sewerage in vain. Quarantine was proposed; commerce frowned. A plan was offered for daily flushing the city's innumerable open street-gutters; it was rejected. The vice of burying in tombs above ground in the heart of town was shown; but the burials went on.

As the year 1853 drew near, a climax of evil conditions seemed to be approached. The city became more dreadfully unclean than before. The scavenging was being tried on a contract system, and the "foul and nauseous steams" from gutters, alleys, and dark nooks became intolerable. In the merchants' interest Carondelet basin and canal were being once more dug out; the New Canal was being widened; gas and water mains were being extended; in the Fourth District, Jackson Street and St. Charles Avenue were being excavated for the road-beds of their railways. In the Third District, many small draining trenches were being dug.

On the 12th of March, the ship *Augusta* sailed from Bremen for New Orleans with upward of two hundred emigrants. Thirteen days afterward the *Northampton* left Liverpool, bound in the same direction, with between three and four hundred Irish. She had sickness on board during the voyage, and some deaths. The *Augusta* had none. While these were on their way, the bark *Siri*, in the port of Rio de Janeiro, lost her captain and several of her crew by yellow fever, and afterward sailed for New Orleans. The ship *Camboden Castle* cleared from Kingston, Jamaica, for the same port, leaving seven of her crew dead of the fever. On the 9th of May, the *Northampton* and the *Siri* arrived in the Mississippi. The *Northampton* was towed to the city alone, and on the 10th was moored at a wharf in the Fourth District, at the head of Josephine Street. The *Siri* was towed up in company with another vessel, the *Saxon*. She was dropped at a wharf in the First District. The *Saxon* moved on and rested some distance away, at a wharf opposite the waterworks reservoir, in front of Market Street. The *Northampton* was found to be very foul. Hands sent aboard to unload and clean her left on the next day, believing they had detected "black vomit" in her hospital. One of them fell sick of yellow fever three days after, but recovered. A second force was employed; several became ill; this was on the 17th. On the same day, the *Augusta* and the *Camboden Castle* entered the harbor in the same tow. The *Camboden Castle* was moored alongside the *Saxon*. At the next wharf, two or three hundred feet below, lay abreast the *Niagara* and the *Harvest Queen*. The *Augusta* passed on up and cast off her tow-lines only when she was moored close to the *Northampton*. The emigrants went ashore. Five thousand landed in New Orleans that year. Here, then, was every condition necessary to the outbreak of a pestilence, whether indigenous, imported, or both.

On the same day that the fever broke out on the *Northampton* it appeared also on the *Augusta*. About the same time it showed itself in one or two distant parts of the city without discernible connection with the shipping. On the 29th, it appeared on the *Harvest Queen*, and, five days later, on the *Saxon*. The *Niagara* had put to sea; but, on the 8th, the fever broke out on her and carried off the captain and a number of the crew. Two fatal cases in the town the attending physician reported under a disguised term, "not wishing to create alarm." Such was the inside, hidden history of the Great Epidemic's beginning.

On the 27th of May, one of the emigrants from the *Northampton* was brought to the charity hospital. He had been four days ill, and he died the next day, of yellow fever. The Board of Health made official report of the case; but the daily papers omitted to publish it. Other reports followed in June; they were shunned in the same way, and the great city, with its one hundred and fifty-four thousand people, one in every ten of whom was to die that year, remained in slumberous ignorance of the truth. It was one of the fashions. On the 2d of July, twenty-five deaths from yellow fever were reported for the closing week. Many "fever centres" had been developed. Three or four of them pointed, for their origin, straight back to the *Northampton ;* one to the *Augusta*, and one to the *Saxon*.

A season of frequent heavy rains, alternating with hot suns and calms—the worst of conditions—set in. At the end of the next week, fifty-nine deaths were reported. There had not been less, certainly, than three hundred cases, and the newspapers slowly and one by one began to admit the presence of danger. But the truth was already

guessed, and alarm and dismay lurked everywhere. Not
in every breast, however; there were still those who
looked about with rather impatient surprise, and—often
in Creole accent, and often not—begged to be told what
was the matter. The deaths around them, they insisted,
in print, were at that moment "fewer in number than in
any other city of similar population in the Union."

Indeed, the fever was still only prowling distantly in
those regions most shunned by decent feet and clean robes;
about Rousseau Street, and the like, along the Fourth
District river-front, where the forlorner German immigrants boarded in damp and miry squalor; in the places
where such little crowded living as there was in the town
was gathered; Lynch's Row and other blocks and courts
in the filthy Irish quarters of St. Thomas and Tchoupitoulas streets; and the foul, dark dens about the French
market and the Mint, in the old French quarter; among
the Gascon *vacheries* and *boucheries*, of repulsive unclean-
ness, on the upper and rear borders of the Fourth District; and around Gormley's Basin—a small artificial harbor at the intersection of Dryades Walk and Felicity Road,
for the wood-cutters and shingle-makers of the swamp,
and "a pestilential muck-and-mire pool of dead animals
and filth of every kind."

But suddenly the contagion leaped into the midst of
the people. In the single week ending July 16th, two
hundred and four persons were carried to the cemeteries.
A panic seized the town. Everywhere porters were toss-

ing trunks into wagons, carriages rattling over the stones and whirling out across the broad white levee to the steamboats' sides. Foot-passengers were hurrying along the sidewalk, luggage and children in hand, and out of breath, many a one with the plague already in his pulse. The fleeing crowd was numbered by thousands.

During the following week, the charity hospital alone received from sixty to one hundred patients a day. Its floors were covered with the sick. From the 16th to the 23d, the deaths averaged sixty-one a day. Presently, the average ran up to seventy-nine. The rains continued, with much lightning and thunder. The weather became tropical; the sun was scorching hot and the shade chilly. The streets became heavy with mud, the air stifling with bad odors, and the whole town a perfect Constantinople for foulness.

August came on. The week ending the 6th showed one hundred and eighty-seven deaths from *other* diseases, an enormous death-rate, to which the fever added nine hundred and forty-seven victims. For a week, the deaths in the charity hospital—where the poor immigrants lay—had been one every half hour.

The next day two hundred and twenty-eight persons died. The pestilence had attacked the Creoles and the blacks. In every direction were confusion, fright, flight, calls for aid, the good "Howards" hurrying from door to door, widows and orphans weeping, till the city was, as an eye-witness says, a "theatre of horrors."

"Alas," cried one of the city journals, "we have not even grave-diggers!" Five dollars an hour failed to hire enough of them. Some of the dead went to the tomb still with pomp and martial honors; but the city scavengers, too, with their carts, went knocking from house to house asking if there were any to be buried. Long rows of coffins were laid in furrows scarce two feet deep, and hurriedly covered with a few shovelfulls of earth, which the daily rains washed away, and the whole mass was left, "filling the air far and near with the most intolerable pestilential odors." Around the grave-yards funeral trains jostled and quarrelled for place, in an air reeking with the effluvia of the earlier dead. Many "fell to work and buried their own dead." Many sick died in carriages and carts. Many were found dead in their beds, in stores, in the streets. Vice and crime broke out fiercely : the police were never so busy. Heroism, too, was seen on every hand. Hundreds toiled for the comfort of sick and dying, and hundreds fell victims to their own noble self-abnegation. Forty-five distant cities and towns sent relief.

On one day, the 11th of August, two hundred and three persons died of the fever. In the week ending two days later, the total deaths were fourteen hundred and ninety-four. Rain fell every day for two months. Streets became so bad that hearses could scarcely reach the cemeteries. On the 20th, the week's mortality was fifteen hundred and thirty-four.

Despair now seemed the only reasonable frame of mind.

In the sky above, every new day brought the same merciless conditions of atmosphere. The earth below bubbled with poisonous gases. Those who would still have fled the scene saw no escape. To leave by ship was to court the overtaking stroke of the plague beyond the reach of medical aid, and probably to find a grave in the sea; while to escape to inland towns was to throw one's self into the arms of the pestilence, carried there by earlier fugitives. The numbers of the dead give but an imperfect idea of the wide-spread suffering and anguish. The disease is repulsive and treacherous, and requires the most unremitting and laborious attention. Its fatal ending is inexpressibly terrible, often attended with raving madness. Among the Creoles of the old French quarter, a smaller proportion than one in each eleven suffered attack. But in the Fourth District, where the unacclimated were most numerous, there were whole wards where more than half the population had to take their chances of life and death from the dreadful contagion. In the little town of Algiers, just opposite the city, a thirty-sixth of all its people died in one week.

On the 22d day of August, the climax was at last reached. Death struck that day, from midnight to midnight, a fresh victim every five minutes, and two hundred and eighty-three deaths summed up an official record that was confessedly incomplete. The next day, there were twenty-five less. The next, thirty-six less than this. Each day was better than the preceding. The crisis had passed. Hope rose into rejoicing. The 1st of September showed but one hundred and nineteen deaths, and the 10th but eighty. North winds and cool, dry weather set in. On the 20th, there were but forty-nine deaths; on the 30th, only sixteen. In some of the inland towns it was still raging, and so continued until the middle of October.

In the cemeteries of New Orleans, between the 1st of June and the 1st of October, nearly eleven thousand persons were buried. To these must be added the many buried without certificate, the hundreds who perished in their flight, and the multitudes who fell in the towns to which the pestilence was carried. It lingered through autumn, and disappeared only in December. During the year 1853 nearly thirty thousand residents of New Orleans were ill of the yellow fever, and there died, from all causes, nearly sixteen thousand.

In the next two summers, 1854 and '55, the fever returned and destroyed more than five thousand persons. Cholera added seventeen hundred and fifty. The two years' death-rates were seventy-two and seventy-three per thousand. That of 1853 was one hundred and eleven. In three years, thirty-seven thousand people had died, and wherever, by ordinary rate of mortality, there should have been one grave or sepulchre, there were four. One can but draw a sigh of relief in the assurance that this is a history of the past, not the present, and that new conditions have made it next to impossible that it should ever be repeated in the future.

The Dead Church
4/ 1884
New Orleans.

XXXIX.

BRIGHTER SKIES.

"OUT of this nettle, danger," says the great bard, "we
pluck this flower, safety." The dreadful scourge
of 1853 roused the people of New Orleans, for the first
time, to the necessity of knowing the proven truth concerning themselves and the city in which they dwelt.

In the midst of the epidemic, the city council had ad-
journed, and a number of its members had fled. But, in
response to popular demand, a board of health had appointed the foremost advocates of quarantine and municipal cleansing a commission to study and report the mel-

ancholy lessons of the plague. It labored arduously for
many months. At its head was that mayor of New Orleans, Crossman by name, whose fame for wise and pro-
tracted rule is still a pleasant tradition of the city, and
whose characteristic phrase—" a great deal to be said on
both sides "—remains the most frequent quotation on the
lips of the common people to-day. Doctors Barton, Axson, McNeil, Symonds, and Riddell,—men at the head of
the medical profession,—completed the body. They were
bold and faithful, and they effected a revolution.

The thinking and unbiased few, who in all communities
must first receive and fructify the germ of truth, were
convinced. The technical question of the fever's conta-
giousness remained unsettled; but its transportability was
fearfully proven in a multitude of interior towns, and its
alacrity in seeking foul quarters and its malignancy there
were plainly shown by its history in the city. The commission pronounced in favor of quarantine, and it was permanently established, and has ever since become, annually,
more and more effective. They earnestly recommended,
also, the purging of the city, and keeping it purged, by
proper drainage and sewerage, of all those foul conditions
that were daily poisoning its earth and air. The response
to this was extremely feeble.

It would seem as if the commercial value both of quarantine and cleanliness might have been seen by the merchant, since the aggregate value of exports, imports, and
domestic receipts fell off twenty-two and a half millions,

and did not entirely recover for three years. But it was not. The merchants, both Creole and American, saw only the momentary inconveniences and losses of quarantine and its defective beginnings; the daily press, in bondage to the merchant through its advertising columns, carped and cavilled in two languages at the innovation and expanded on the filthiness of other cities, while the general public thought what they read.

Yet, in the face of all set-backs, the city that once was almost annually scourged, has, in the twenty-seven years since the Great Epidemic, which virtually lasted till 1855, suffered but one mild and three severe epidemics. In 1878, occurred the last of these, and the only severe one in fourteen years. Its fatality was but little over half as great as that of the Great Epidemic. In the five years ending with 1855, the average annual mortality had been seventy. In the next five, it fell to forty-five. In the five of the secession and war period, it was forty. In the next, it was thirty-nine; in the next, it sank to thirty-four and a half; in that which closed in 1880, notwithstanding the terrible epidemic of 1878, the rate was but thirty-three and a half, and in the five years since that affliction it was under twenty-seven.

The popular idea that a sudden revolution in the sanitary affairs of the Creole city was effected by General B. F. Butler in 1862 is erroneous. It has just been shown that the city's health had already been greatly improved before the Civil War set in. When General Butler assumed control of its affairs there had been no epidemic of yellow fever for four years. The year of his domination was actually less healthy than the year before, its death-rate being thirty-six, against thirty-four for 1861. In the second summer of Federal occupation the rate was an entire third larger than in the summer before the city fell. No five years since the close of the war, dividing the time off in regular periods of that length, has failed thus far to show a better mortality-rate than that five which ended with 1865 ; and in ten of the eighteen years immediately following that of Butler's notorious rule, the mortality has been lighter than it was that year. The mortality of 1879 was under twenty-four, and that of 1880, twenty-six per thousand.

The events of 1878 are fresh in the public mind. In New Orleans they overwhelmed the people at large with the convictions which 1853 had impressed upon the more thoughtful few. To the merchant, "shot-gun quarantines" throughout the Southern Mississippi Valley explained themselves. The commercial necessity of quarantine and sanitation was established without a single scientific light, and measures were taken in hand for perfecting both— measures which are growing and bearing fruit day by day. They have already reduced the insalubrity of New Orleans to a point where it may be compared, though timidly, with that of other great cities, and promise before long to make the city, really and emphatically, the home of health, comfort, and safety.

In the study of his expanded city, we have wandered
from the contemplation of the Creole himself.   It remains
to be said that, unquestionably, as his town has expanded
and improved, so has he.   As the improvements of the
age draw the great world nearer and nearer to him, he
becomes more and more open to cosmopolitan feeling.
The hostility to Americans, as such, is little felt.   The
French tongue is falling into comparative disuse, even in
the family circle.   The local boundaries are overstepped.
He lives above Canal Street now without feeling exiled.
The social circles blend into each other.   Sometimes, with
the old Gallic intrepidity of conviction, he moves ahead
of the American in progressive thought.

In these matters of sanitary reform, he has his share—
or part of it.   The old feeling of castellated immunity in
his own high-fenced home often resents, in sentiment at
least, official house-to-house inspection and the disturbance
of a state of affairs under which his father and grandfather
reached a good old age and left no end of children.   Yet
the movement in general has his assent ; sometimes his
co-operation ; sometimes his subscription ; and his doctors
take part in debates and experiments.   He is in favor of
all this healthful flushing ; this deepening and curbing of
canals ; this gratuitous and universal distribution of copperas, etc.   Against one feature only he wages open war.
He laughs, but he is in earnest; copperas, he tolerates ;
lime, the same ; all odorless disinfectants, indeed ; but
carbolic acid—no !   In Gallic fierceness, he hurls a nick-

name at it—"*acide diabolique*." When he smells it, he loads his gun and points it through his shutters. You shall never sprinkle him with that stuff—never! And who knows but he is nearest to the right?

On his sugar plantations, in the parishes named for the saints, he has grown broad and robust—a strong, manly figure in neat, spurred boots, a refined blood flushing through his bronzed but delicate skin, making him at times even florid. He is not so mortgaged as he used to be. Yankee neighbors have dropped in all about him lately, as they did in earlier days about his city cousins; some from the eastern, some from the western North—he calls them all by one generic term. But he likes them. They are preferable to "Cadians"—much. They stimulate him. He is not so wedded to "open kettle" sugars as he once was. He is putting "vacuum pans" into his sugar-house—nay, did not the Creole, Valcour-Aime, introduce the vacuum pan into Louisiana?—and studies chemistry till he beats his breast in the wholeness of his attention. Yet he is full, too, of the questions of the day. The candor with which he grasps the new turn of affairs resulting from the Civil War is worthy of imitation by many an Anglo-American Southern community. He is apt to say he never did believe heartily in African slavery and now he knows it was a sad mistake. The cruel sentiments of caste that sprang from it still survive, but they burn with no fierceness. They cannot easily perish, for they have been handed down through generations. They are like those old bronze Argands, once so highly prized, still standing, rayless, on his mantelpiece; lamps without oil. You may still see Congo Square, where the slave once danced his savage African songs in tattered half-

The Old Calaboza.

nakedness on Sabbath afternoons; but the thunder of African drums rumbles there no more, and the Creole and the freedman are alike well pleased that "the jig is up." The Calaboza remains, but the irons that once burnt the flower-de-luce into the recaptured runaway's shoulder, and the four whipping-posts to which the recalcitrant slave was once made fast by hands and feet, are gone, and the Creole is glad of it. He is willing to be just to his former bondservant, now fellow-citizen, and where he holds the old unjust attitudes does so with little consciousness. The old Gallic intrepidity of thought comes to his aid, and is helping him out of the fiercely extreme conservatism engendered by an institution that could not afford to entertain suggestions of change. There is no other part of Louisiana where the slave has made so much progress, as a mass, toward the full possession of freedom as he has in the " sugar parishes." The colored man's history in the land of the Creoles we cannot write here. It would throw light upon our theme, but——some other time. It is a theme by itself, too large to be hung upon this. Later, the Creole himself will be more prepared for it. Meantime he quotes the New York papers, and tells you frankly that he only wishes he could be rid of North Louisiana—where the " American " planter reigns supreme—it is so behind the times.

When he is not so he is very different. In such case he bows his head to fate. His fences are broken ; his levee is dangerous ; the plastering is falling in his parlor ; his garden has become a wild, damp grove, weed-grown and untrodden ; his sugar is dark, his thin linen coat is home-made ; he has transferred his hopes to rice and made his home sickly with irrigation ; he doesn't care who you are, and will not sell a foot of his land—no, not for price that man can name !—till the red flag hangs out for him on

An Inner Court—Royal Street.

the courthouse square and the man with one drumstick drums him out of house and home.

In New Orleans, sad shrinkages in the value of down-town property have played havoc with the old Creole *rentier*. Court officers and lawyers are full of after-dinner stories illustrating the pathetic romance of his fate. He keeps at home, on the front veranda. His wife and daughter take in sewing and make orange marmalade and fig preserves on small private contracts. His son is a lounger in the court-rooms. The young man buttons his worn coat tightly about his small waist, walks with a brisk affectation of being pressed for time, stops you silently in Royal Street or Père Antoine's Alley, on the stairway of the old Cabildo, to light his cigarette from your cigar—symbolic action, always lighting his cigarette from somebody's cigar—gives you a silent, call-it-square sort of bow as full of grace as a Bourbon prince's, and hurries on, hoping soon to become fifth assistant to some deputy sheriff or public surveyor, or, if he have influential relatives, runner for a bank. He "plays the lottery," that curse of his town.

"Well, of co'se," he says, blowing the tobacco smoke through his nose, "thaz the way with evveybody, those time'—sinz ladely." Really he would ask you around to "The Gem," but—his poor, flat pocket! nothing in it but his "memo'andum book," and not even a "memo'andum" in that.

But he has kinsmen, in goodly number, who blush for him; he will tell you so with a strange mixture of pride and humility; and who are an honor and a comfort to their beloved city. They sit on the most important committees in the great Cotton Exchange, and in the Produce Ex-

Old Spanish Gateway and Stair in the Cabildo.

change, and in reform movements. They are cashiers and vice-presidents and presidents of street railway companies, of insurance companies, of banks. They stand in the front ranks at the bar. They gain fame and rever-

ence on the bench. They have held every office within
the gift of the State. And they have been great beyond
their own boundaries—out in the great world. A Louisiana Creole was once, for a short time, Minister of War in
France, under the Directory. Another sat in the Spanish
Cortes. Another became a Spanish Lieutenant-General.
Another was a general of patriot forces when the South
American provinces threw off the yoke of Spain. Jean
Jacques Audubon was a Creole of Louisiana. Louis Gotts-
chalk was a New Orleans Creole. General Beauregard
is a Creole of an old Creole line.

They are *not* "dying out." Why should they? "Doze
climade sood dem" better than it suits any alien who has
ever tried the drowsy superabundance of its summer sunlight, and they are becoming ever more and more worthy
to survive. Their pride grows less fierce, their courage is
no weaker for it, their courtesy is more cordial, they are
more willing to understand and be understood, and their
tastes for moral and intellectual refinements are growing.

Even in their headlong gayeties—the spectacular pa-
geants of the carnival—they have stricken hands with the
" American," borrowed his largeness of pretension and the
barbaric ambition of the South's retarded artistic impulse.
The unorganized rout of masks peculiar to the old Latin
cities has been turned into gorgeous, not to say gaudy,
tableaux drawn through the streets under the glare of
blazing petroleum and frequent lime-lights, on tinselled
cars, by draped teams, to the blare of brass music and the

roar of popular acclamation, in representation of one or
another of the world's great myths, epics, or episodes.
Many thousands of people are drawn from contiguous or
distant parts, with the approach of each Mardi-gras, to see
—may the good town forgive the term—these striding
puerilities. Some come to gaze in wonder on these mira-
cles in *papier-maché* and plaster-of-Paris, and some, it is
feared, to smile behind their hats at make-believe art,
frivolous taste, and short-sighted outlay. The expenditure
of time, money, and labor on these affairs is great—
worthy of more lasting achievements. One Carnival day
and night some years ago the crowds were more enormous
than ever, the displays were gorgeous, the whole city was
one wide revel. All through the hours of a glorious day
the long, dazzling procession passed with their jewelled king
sparkling in their midst, in street-full after street-full of
multitudes that made the warm air quiver with acclama-
tions. Night fell, and Comus and his Krewe came forth
in a blaze of torches and made everything seem tame that
had gone before ; and when at midnight, with the tinkle of
a little bell, all disappeared, the people said that there had
never been such a carnival. But when the sun rose again
they prayed there might never be just such another. For on
his neglected couch, sought too tardily, the victim of over-
fatigue, the royal Comus, lay dead. The "American,"
as well as the Creole, owns an undivided half of this folly,
and the Creole, as well as the "American," is beginning
to deprecate it. Already better aspirations are distinctly

shown, and the city's efforts are reaching forth in many directions to adorn herself with attractions that do not vanish at cockcrow, but, inviting the stranger to become a visitor, also tempt him to remain, a resident.

We have said that the air which the Creole breathes with unvarying satisfaction and exhales in praises of its superior merits is never very hot or very cold, by the mercury. Even in July and August the column lingers, for the most part, under 95°, and in mid-winter seldom sinks more than four or five degrees below the freezing-point. But since it is the evaporation from the surrounding swamps, marshes, and other shallow waters that makes this moderation, the effects upon the person are those of decidedly greater extremes of heat and cold. Yet the long and dazzlingly beautiful summers are generally salubrious, and it would be difficult to exaggerate the charms of the exuberant spring which sets in before January is gone, and rises gently in fervor until May ushers in the summer. As to the summer, it goes, unwillingly, in November.

Its languid airs have induced in the Creole's speech great softness of utterance. The relaxed energies of a luxurious climate find publication, as it were, when he turns final *k* into *g ;* changes *th,* and *t* when not initial, to *d ;* final *p* to *b,* drops initial *h,* final *le,* and *t* after *k ;* often, also, the final *d* of past tenses ; omits or distorts his *r,* and makes a languorous *z* of all *s*'s and soft *c*'s except initials. On the other hand, the old Gallic alertness and wire-edge still asserts itself in the confusing and inter-

changing of long *e* and short *i*—sheep for ship, and ship
for sheep—in the flattening of long *i*, as if it were coming
through cane-crushers, in the prolonging of long *a*, the
intrusion of uncalled-for initial *h*'s, and the shortening and
narrowing of nearly all long and broad vowels.

The African slave in Louisiana—or, it may be more
correct to say, in St. Domingo, before coming to Louisiana—corrupted the French tongue as grossly, or even
more so, than he did the English in the rice plantations of
South Carolina. No knowledge of scholarly French is a
guarantee that the stranger will understand the " Creole "
negro's *gombo*. To the Creole *sang pur* this dialect is an
inexhaustible fountain of amusement. In the rural parishes the harsh archaisms of the Acadian perform the
same office and divide the Creole's attention. But in " the
City " they Acadian dialect is hardl known, and for a century or more the melodious drollery and grotesqueness of
the negro *patois* has made it the favorite vehicle of humor-
ous song and satirical prose and verse.[1]

---

[1] In Le Carillon, " Journal Hebdomadaire, organe des populations
Franco-Louisianaises, Bureaux, 125 Rue Royale," appeared in 1874 a
series of witty political lampoons, from one of which a few lines may be
drawn by way of illustration.

Miché Carillon,

Y a quéques jours mo té apé fouillé mo champ pistaches, et vous va
connin, y a rien comme fouillé pistaches pour gagnin zidées. Et jour-
là mo té plein zidées. Mo té lire bo matin la que nous té apé couri
gagnin eine nouvelle élection, et mo cœur té batte si fort à nouvelle-là
que mo té bo Man Cribiche quatre fois et Man Magritte trois fois, en

It would make a long chapter to untangle its confused mass of abbreviations, suppressions of inflections, *liasons*, nazalizations, omissions, inversions, startling redundancies, and original idioms. The Creole does not tolerate its use in polite conversation, and he is probably seldom aware that his English sparkles and crackles with the same pretty corruptions. For example, or as the Creole himself would say, "faw egzamp," let us take the liberty of inventing a sentence and setting it in his lips :

"I am going to do my utmost to take my uncle there, but he is slightly paralyzed and I do not think he will feel like going."——He would say—

"I goin' do my possib' fedge ma hunc' yond', bud, 'owevva, 'e's a lit' bit pa'a*lyze* an' I thing 'e don' goin' fill *ligue.*"

Examples need not be multiplied. One innocent assertion that found its way to a page of the present writer's scanty notes from the lips of a Creole country physician will stand for a hundred. The doctor, like many of his race, would have known at once that the foregoing illustration was bad English ; but he is not aware, to this day, that there was any inaccuracy in his own simple assertion :

---

m'écriant : "Oh ! mes femmes ! mes épouses ! vous va zétes bientôt pétète Liétnantes-Gouverneuses."

*   *   *   *   *   *   *   *

Jour-là, yé té oulé fait sauté Mechanic's avec tous so mécaniques, yé té pas capabe connin où Antouène té passé, yé trouvé li, lendemain matin, li té attaché après so maillet et li té apé dit : "O reine Voudoux, sauvez le Liétnant-Gouvernair,—" etc.

" I've juz been pulling some teeth to your neighbor."

There are reasons—who can deny it ?—why we should be glad that the schoolmaster is abroad in Louisiana, teaching English. But the danger is, that somewhere in the future lurks a day when the Creole will leave these loveable drolleries behind him, and speak our tongue with the same dull correctness with which it is delivered in the British House of Lords. May he live long, and that time be very, very far away !

THE END.